RISING
FROM THE
DUST

FAUZA BELTZ

RISING FROM THE DUST

A Woman's Journey to Self-Discovery

Disclaimer

TITLE: Rising From the Dust: A Woman's Journey to Self-Discovery

AUTHOR: Fauza Beltz

WEBSITE www.fauzabeltz.com

The moral rights of Fauza Beltz to be identified as the author of this work have been asserted in accordance with the Copyright Act 1968.

First published in Australia 2016.

Any opinions expressed in this work are exclusively those of the author and are not necessarily the views held or endorsed by the publisher.

All rights reserved. No part of this publication may be reproduced or transmitted by any means, electronic, photocopying or otherwise, without prior written permission of the author.

All of the information, techniques, skills and concepts contained within this publication are of the nature of general comment only, and are not in any way recommended as individual advice. The intent is to offer a variety of information to provide a wider range of choices, now and in the future, recognising that we all have widely diverse circumstances and viewpoints. Should any reader choose to make use of the information herein, this is their decision, and the author and publisher/s do not assume any responsibilities whatsoever under any conditions or circumstances. The author does not take responsibility for the business, financial, personal or other success, results or fulfilment upon the readers' decision to use this information. It is recommended that the readers obtain their own independent advice.

Creator: Beltz, Fauza, author.

Title: Rising From the Dust: A Woman's Journey to Self-Discovery / Fauza Beltz

ISBN: 9780994593801 (paperback)

Target Audience: For young adults Subjects:

Subjects:

Beltz, Fauza.
Beltz, Fauza -- Childhood and Youth
Muslim women -- Biography
Successful people -- Biography
Self-actualization (Psychology) in women

Women in development -- Kenya

Dewey Number: 305.4092

Published by Nkandu Beltz

DEDICATION

Dedicated to all the strong women around the globe who have crawled through the dust and have come out on the other side full of power and self-acceptance.

*With lots of love
and kindness.*

RISING FROM THE **DUST**

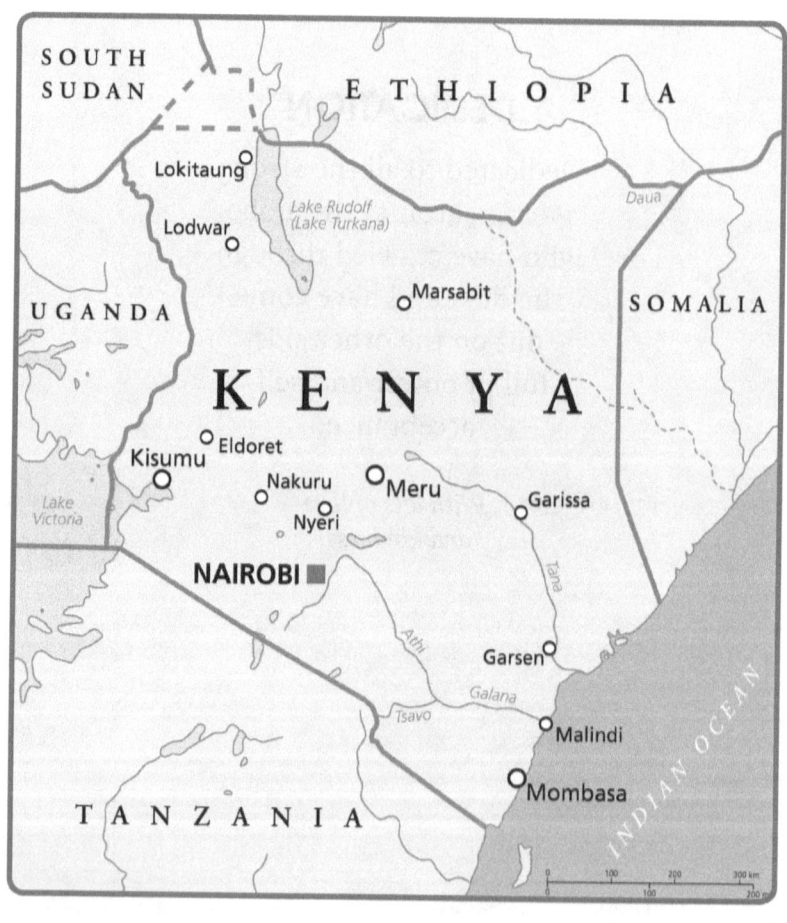

ACKNOWLEDGEMENTS

I really hope that I do not forget anyone, and just in case I do, please know that you have a special place in my heart.

I will start with Ms Nkandu Beltz. Words cannot describe how grateful I am to have you in my life, and you have always reminded me that I have the power to be who I want to be. You are such an inspiration and I love your work and the energy you display. Huge thanks for helping me to bring this manuscript to life.

To my personal coach, Amanda van den Berk-van den Berg. Many thanks for always guiding me to find my true uniqueness.

Thank you also to Pauline Charles for working on my website.

Thank you so much, Nuri Septina, for creating my book cover: you exceeded my expectations.

To Maria Pearson and Klaus Miserra from grow.ME, thank you so much for all the empowerment, knowledge and guidance that I learned from you during the Ro'Ya business workshops in 2015. It is through this experience that I fully understand what it is to be a woman in business.

To Nadine Halabi and the whole management of Dubai Business Women Council, many thanks for giving me the chance to be one of the Ro'Ya participants for 2015.

To my childhood friend Bernice. Thank you for riding on with me, you have always reminded me that no matter what happens in life, we can always look back and be grateful for everything, good or bad, for it has taught us that we should love a little more.

RISING FROM THE DUST

To Renato Nicdao and Chris Fuentes, thank you for the gorgeous picture that I chose for the book cover.

To Ann Nyambura, thank you for your guidance.

To my husband Dolf, you are my anchor, my inspiration and my support. God bless you for your love.

To my darling Jasper, thank you for teaching me what true love is. I love you.

My sincere gratitude to the divine providence for my many blessings: Your grace, Your favour, Your wisdom, Your unconditional love and for my salvation.

FOREWORD

Fauza is one of those very special people in life who instantly makes a great impact when you meet them. From the time she stepped into my office, following her pursuit of emotional fulfillment and her goals, she leapt with dazzling speed into her coaching journey and process. During this journey, she impressed me with her awareness and willingness to go deeper and deeper, being wildly curious while, at the same time, conquering her fears, doubts and her many questions. For me as a coach, this is so beautiful to see in a person. It is such an honor for me to guide someone who is so willing and ready to take on the journey, it's magical!

Fauza is a determined, loving, caring young woman who encourages and inspires other women about the power of sharing and who invites them to speak up, easing their pain.

As a reader, be inspired by her strength, endurance, love and her refusal to give up! This is an empowering story of her young self bravely following her authentic path. It is a true-life story of resilience and bouncing back with a zest for life to overcome obstacles. Fauza is a woman who knows herself… let her inspire you too!

Now shine, Fauza, and pass it on!

With love,

Amanda van den Berk- van den Berg, CPCC
Certified Professional Co-Active Coach
Personal Development Coach and Mentor

'For there is hope for a tree, if it be cut down, that it will sprout again, and that its shoots will not cease. Though its root grow old in the earth, and its stump die in the soil, yet at the scent of water it will bud and put out branches like a young plant.'

Job 14:7

INTRODUCTION

'Loving ourselves through the process of owning our story is the bravest thing we'll ever do.'

Brene Brown

I do not consider myself a writer but I have always wanted to put something together to share a bit of my life story with you. For many years I have been praying and struggling about writing my book. This dream has been fermenting for many years until recently.

Sometimes we want to do things but we don't know how to start or who to go to and get help. This can be a massive dilemma.

The wakeup call came after my story was featured in Nkandu Beltz's book, *Fierce and Fabulous: The Feminine Force of Success*, which is a collection of stories from 15 women in Australia, New Zealand and the United Arab Emirates. Ms Beltz was investigating the feminine force of success and why these women didn't give up when life got tough. Instead, they bounced back and created businesses that help other women to flourish.

When I got this opportunity, I was scared at first. I wasn't sure how people would relate to my story. It was only after attending the first *Fierce and*

RISING FROM THE DUST

Fabulous book launch at Dymocks in Sydney in February 2016 that I really wanted to compile something more on paper. I remember speaking about why I had decided to be a part of the book. I felt like people had connected with me. They were very attentive and wanted to know what had happened in my life.

Two weeks after the book launch, I received messages from some of the people in that audience who had read my story and told me how it had resonated with their lives. It made me really feel grateful that I had inspired a few people and the urge to put something more in writing started to creep in again.

After a few conversations with Nkandu, the journey of writing my book started. It has been a struggle putting these words together to make this book readable. I have been through a lot of emotional moments. I have cried, I have laughed and sometimes I have wanted to give up. This is because I was going back to the old buried memories, which I didn't want to think about. But to understand my whole story, those memories had to be unlocked, otherwise the story would not be balanced.

Writing this book was a true labour of love. There are stories from my early childhood years in Kwale, Kenya, to my teenage time in Nairobi and some stories from more recent events, plus so much more. I am so grateful to you for going on this journey with me and I truly hope you all enjoy reading this book as much as I did writing it. It is my sincere hope that you get a lot of value from this book. When life gets hard, you know that I have been in a similar situation and always have faith and hope that everything will be okay. My journey has not been easy but I have learned to be strong and to stand in my own power. If you know someone who is struggling, I encourage you to pass this book to him or her. It's through sharing our stories and learning from other people that we learn to be strong.

Fauza Beltz

CONTENTS

Acknowledgments

Foreword

Introduction

Preface   3

Chapter One:	The Untold Stories of Triumphs and Tragedies	7
Chapter Two:	The Magical Land of Kenya	17
Chapter Three:	My Teenage Years	23
Chapter Four:	The Power of Discovering	31
Chapter Five:	Becoming Truly Independent	41
Chapter Six:	Choose Wisely	51
Chapter Seven:	Acceptance and Forgiveness	59
Chapter Eight:	Searching for One's Happiness	69
Chapter Nine:	Trust Your Gut Instinct	77
Chapter Ten:	Becoming Empowered	83
Chapter Eleven:	Choosing a Career	89
Chapter Twelve:	Finding True Love	93
Chapter Thirteen:	My Expat Life in Dubai	97
Chapter Fourteen:	The Importance of Mentors	107
Chapter Fifteen:	Be Open to New Opportunities	111
Chapter Sixteen:	Inspiring Women	115
Chapter Seventeen:	Meeting Dr John Demartini	119
Epilogue		125
Bonus Chapter	Fierce and Fabulous	127

A PERSONAL NOTE FROM THE PUBLISHER

To the reader,

As the Founder, Director and CEO of AscendSmart Publishing, I make it part of my practice to offer you a personal review of the authors we publish. The reason is to give you a deeper understanding of what this book is about and the impact it will have on your life.

Fauza is my sister-in-law and one of the most amazing people I know. I have been inspired by the resilience and determination that she possesses, despite all the hardships she has gone through. This goes to show that it's not how hard you hit the ground when you fall, but how fast you get up and what attitude you choose to go with.

Fauza has done so with grace and style while helping many people along the way. You will discover just how powerful you are and that your past does not define your future. I hope you will enjoy this read as much as I did and wish you all the success with your life and business.

With love,
Nkandu
xoxo

PREFACE

'If you are tired of living on the beaten path that everyone else walks on all the time, then venture into the woods. Some people would be afraid they would get lost but a confident woman expects to have a new experience that might be outrageously wonderful.'

Joyce Mayer, The Confident Woman

This is a life story of a woman who has managed to take the negative and turn every situation into a life-learning journey.

One thing that I have learned in my life journey is that it is by sharing our stories that we get to heal ourselves. I believe it is by doing so that we are able to heal other people too. When you tell your story, you are freeing yourself and give other people permission to acknowledge their own life experiences and love themselves along the way.

I believe in the power of love. There is power in loving yourself. I don't see the value of getting depressed or feeling powerless. You gain power and confidence from being willing to go out into the world and see what you can do. You might not always accomplish your goals, but you have to maintain your faith and self-belief. You can't help yourself or others if you look inward and feel sorry for yourself.

I believe that we have to change our ways of looking at challenges so that we can go out and help other people.

All of our life journeys are different and no matter how difficult or challenging they seem, they are temporary situations. It is only when we accept what is going on in our lives that we can make those difficult circumstances easier to deal with.

I used to compare myself with other people or my friends whose families of origin were complete. But then I was losing myself or even getting more hurt. Every family has their own emotional upheavals. I believe that it is very common to assume that the grass on the other side of the fence is greener than yours, but so often it is not.

I think it is very important to accept who we are because if we do not love ourselves and accept our own circumstances, we will be living a life of fear and wishing for things that are not necessary. We all have a story to tell but there are only a few people who can actually pick up a pen and a paper to write it down. Often you hear people say, 'I don't want to talk about it because people are going to judge me,' but most people are going through similar journeys or have been there one way or another.

Preface

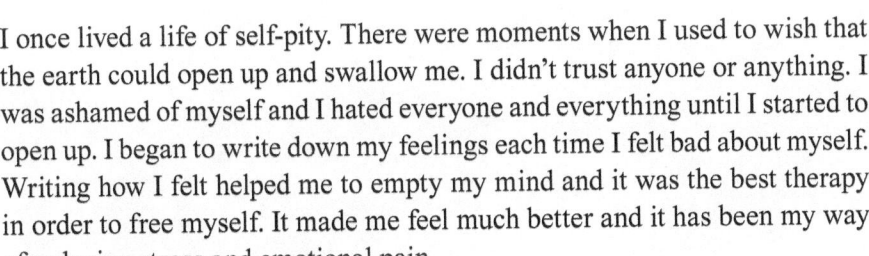

I once lived a life of self-pity. There were moments when I used to wish that the earth could open up and swallow me. I didn't trust anyone or anything. I was ashamed of myself and I hated everyone and everything until I started to open up. I began to write down my feelings each time I felt bad about myself. Writing how I felt helped me to empty my mind and it was the best therapy in order to free myself. It made me feel much better and it has been my way of reducing stress and emotional pain.

When I came up with the idea of sharing my story with others, I was scared. I had the story in my mind but each time I tried to write it down, I found myself stressed. I now fully believe there is nothing wrong with me having written this book as it is. My intention is to share my story with you and when you recognise certain experiences, you realise you are not alone. This book is for you.

Often its people we trust who are the ones to disappoint us. People will always say things about you and label you. Maybe you have done something that you failed at: we all fail at something at some point in our lives. We do make mistakes going through life, but one thing I have learned, no matter how many times we fall, we do get up again.

> 'Many days are wasted comparing ourselves to others and wishing to be something we are not. Everybody has their own strengths and weaknesses and it is only when you accept everything you are and aren't, that you will truly succeed.'
>
> Unknown

'Every child who is conceived is loved by God no matter what circumstances or shame he or she may have brought into the family.'

Fauza Beltz

CHAPTER ONE

The Untold Stories of Triumphs and Tragedies

CHAPTER ONE

The Untold Stories of Triumphs and Tragedies

What does it mean to be born out of wedlock and left to be raised by grandparents?

How does it feel not to be raised by your own father and mother?

The answer is really not clear, although I was that baby who was not planned. But I believe all things work together for the greater good.

Growing up without either parent close to me, I was forced to mature earlier than most other children. Memories of my earlier years as a child are vivid. I was born in a rural area in Tiribe in Kwale in Kenya. Tiribe is a small town in the district of Kwale. Kwale has four topographic features: namely, the coastal plain, the Foot plateau, the coastal uplands and the Nyika plateau. The district is also famous for its white sandy beaches and wild life conservation. It is a true paradise for relaxing and enjoying nature.

I remember very well that my mum and dad were not married. I don't remember living with both of my parents in the same house. I have very few details of their relationship but one thing I know for sure is that I am the only child of the two of them.

Traditionally, a woman is supposed to be married before having children. But my mum became pregnant with me without being married. My mum already had two children from her previous relationship and had been divorced before she met my father.

CHAPTER 1: The Untold Stories of Triumphs and Tragedies

I really do not know how they met, but what I know is that I was conceived on their first intimate encounter. I wouldn't want to think that this was an accident because I am sure God had his own plan for the innocent embryo.

My mum was accused of falling pregnant intentionally and this caused a lot of havoc between my parents' families. After my mother became pregnant with me, her parents sent her to my father's place, which was normal in their culture. When a woman is pregnant and not married she has to go to the man's family.

However, my father could not marry my mum as he did not have a job and my mother was older than he was. It did not help that my mother had two children from her previous failed marriage. Even though my mother was pregnant with his child, my father and his family did not accept these aspects of my mother. The family refused to allow the two to marry.

My mother was therefore forced to go back to her parents to continue her life while she was pregnant with me.

My maternal grandfather was really upset and severely punished my mother for falling pregnant without being accepted by the father of her unborn child. Her family also could not understand why my mum became pregnant when she already had two small boys, one of 1 year and one of 4 years.

RISING FROM THE DUST

'Unlike a drop of water which loses its identity when it joins the ocean, man does not lose his being in the society in which he lives. Man's life is independent. He is born not for the development of the society alone, but for the development of his self.'

B R Ambedkar

Growing up without my parents, I did not fully understand the core of my being. I have spent all my life not knowing who I am, but I have always known who God says I am. I really do not know why there should be a difference between children whose parents are married and living together versus the ones whose parents are not married nor living together. It is something that I have never understood, since the child has nothing to do with the parents' choices and the decisions that adults make. To me, children are innocent and shouldn't be victimized by what has happened between parents since it is not their choice.

This was the beginning of my life as far as I can remember.

Later in my life, after episodes of emotional turmoil, of feeling abandoned and alone as if in a desert without identity and purpose, I had to confront my mother about her past and my feeling of abandonment and lack of affection growing up. Being a mother myself I have realised how beautiful a mother's love is for their children. I only realised the true depth of mother-child love after having my son, Jasper. This realization made me want to reach out to my mum to have a mother-daughter bonding since she never raised me.

I believe that God chose my parents for me, but I have had moments where I have asked myself how and why He chose my parents for me to be in a

CHAPTER 1: The Untold Stories of Triumphs and Tragedies

broken love. Sometimes I wished that I had grown up with my mum and dad together in a complete family. Sometimes I wished that I had never grown up in different homes. As much as I have so many questions with no answers, I know I am alive and there is something that is manifesting in my life, which is God, who knows all the answers to my questions, and one day I will probably understand my life.

I believe we are all connected in one way or another. From as young an age as I can remember I wanted to have answers to all my questions, but now I accept the fact that I cannot have answers for everything.

Talking to my mum, I understand that she had a tough time. Due to the shame that she brought to her family in having a third child and being unmarried to the father of the unborn child, society looked down on her. She stayed with my grandparents until she gave birth to me, after which she took me with her to the city of Mombasa, and left my step brothers with her mother.

Mombasa is a city on the coast of Kenya. It is the nation's largest city after the capital, Nairobi. My mother took a new step in moving to Mombasa to start a new chapter of her life, where she had to work and to take care of herself and her children. She was picking up the pieces of her shattered life and broken family. My mother was doing some basic jobs to provide a living for herself and her kids. As time went by, she fell in love with another man. They got married and a new life for her started to unfold. Her new husband had a job and he could take care of my mum together with my half-brothers and me.

Shortly after marriage, my mother became pregnant again and she gave birth to another boy, my third stepbrother. The birth of my stepbrother changed my life, as my mother could not keep me with her as she had another child from her new man. So, when I turned 3 years old she sent me back to my maternal grandmother who had to raise me further. A new life started for me, although I do not have memories of that time. I do not remember if my mum ever visited me after she sent me back to her mother.

But from then on, my grandmother was in charge of taking care of me. My aunties lived close to my grandmother, so I got lots of attention and as a child everything looked normal. I did the normal things that kids do, like playing in the rain and playing house, using the red mud for baking, activities that were normal growing up in most African communities.

When you are born out of wedlock in an African community, generally you are considered a cursed child and it is a big deal. The society looks at you differently: they look down on you. I am not sure if it is the act of pre-marital sex or the evidence of the child that is considered to be a sin. I believe it is the act is considered the sin, but I am confused as to why the product of the sin is treated the way it is. Is this because the child is evidence of the original sin, or is there some other unclear reason? Whatever, it is only the creator of the universe that knows the truth of it all.

I lived with my grandmother until the age of five. That's when my father instructed his mum - my paternal grandmother - to collect me from my maternal grandmother. Even now I am not sure why my father decided on this, but it was my first understanding that my father was aware of my existence and wanted to take care of me.

I have little memory of the time with my maternal grandmother but, after the change of household, I bonded with my new "mum", my father's mother. I lived with her, sharing the same room, but as far as I can remember, I had my own bed. During the years with my paternal grandmother I did not see my mum, who moved on with her life in a different town. Unfortunately, my father's family was very strict and I was not allowed to visit mum, even when she came over to see her mother.

My dad was not living with us in the countryside as he was working in Nairobi as a police officer. My father always supported his mother and me with food and he provided shelter with the little money he earned as a police officer. He did all that he could to support me.

CHAPTER 1: The Untold Stories of Triumphs and Tragedies

At the age of seven, I started elementary school. I had to walk every morning to go to school with other children from our home area. I would return home in the afternoon, and when I got home I had to do the household chores. It was normal for me to fetch water, cut firewood, and wash my clothes, and also prepare food for my paternal grandmother and me.

There was little time left for playing with other kids.

During the years with my granny, I did not experience what motherly love was, but when I look back, I am very grateful to her for chipping in to be my "mum". She had raised her own children, so she had the skills needed to do the same for her granddaughter. She raised me with the little knowledge that she had, as women of her age never went to school. When I made a mistake, her way of correcting me as a child was by hitting or insulting me. It did not matter who was around: even in front of other kids she would punish me. I have a big scar that reminds me of this period. But even today, I have no idea what exactly happened. I cannot blame her, as this was the only way she knew how to deal with me, but my self-esteem was completely ruined.

I became insecure, withdrawn and afraid in order to try to avoid these punishments. I learned that I had to be fully responsible for what she expected from me even as a child, as that was the only way I could keep ahead of her. As I could not reflect on my life at that moment, I believed the life that I had at that time to be very good because I didn't know anything else other than what granny knew and taught me.

I loved my granny, despite what had been happening in the household. At least, I thought I loved my granny, as she was the only person with whom I lived, so I had nothing to compare with. She was like a mother to me, but as soon as my cousins came to visit, I was no longer important. I didn't understand why, but when I asked I was told that the grandkids from my auntie were more important than I. That sounded strange to me as I thought we were all her grandkids. I started to realise that I was a cursed child, born out of an unacceptable relationship.

My dad moved on with his life in Nairobi and he found the love of his life. I do remember vividly that I attended their wedding as a young girl. I always dreamt my father would marry my mum, but unfortunately, sometimes the things we desire do not come true and life has to move on.

Months later in their marriage they had a new member in the family: my stepsister was born. I was happy as I had someone with whom I shared my father's blood. At that time I did not feel very connected anymore with my mother's children, my stepbrothers. Although we never lived under the same roof, I was so excited to know there was a small (step) sister somewhere in Kenya.

I never lived with my dad and his wife but I was very fortunate to visit them in Nairobi during school holidays. I could stay with them for a month, but when I was about to go back to school I had to return to my granny in the countryside. I had to learn to take each day as it comes and try to make the best of it, but living in the countryside there was nothing much to do, apart from working for granny and myself.

I thought I would be lucky at the primary school as my uncle - my father's brother - was one of the teachers. Instead of it being lucky, it turned out to be the opposite. For every mistake I made, however small, he would beat me using a cane and most of the time it was done during the assembly or even in front of the class. The public humiliation was overwhelming. When I thought that was it, I would get the same punishment again at home. Fear and shame became part of me. I was afraid to make mistakes as I did not want to be punished in front of the other students. I was very unhappy with myself and regretted every single thing I did, because of the fear that whatever I did, some kind of punishment would follow. I was deeply depressed in those days and I never saw any meaning in doing anything for myself as I felt like I was not appreciated and loved. And I only lived day by day.

CHAPTER 1: The Untold Stories of Triumphs and Tragedies

I taught myself not to stay angry and created a big layer of protection around myself, which influenced my personality. I had no one to share my sorrows with as my granny could not do anything as she was afraid of my uncle too. Although she also punished me, she never liked the fact that my uncle would cane me, which to me was an expression of her motherly love as she was the one raising me.

My mum was nowhere to be found and dad lived in Nairobi with his family. Although he visited granny and me during his annual leave, I was not able to talk about my feelings with him, as to do so was not normal in the culture. Also based in the culture is the idea that children are not supposed to challenge adults. In my culture my uncle had the same power as my own father, so for me to tell my father was not allowed and considered to be rude. I had to accept my life as it was.

'Perhaps travel cannot prevent bigotry, but by demonstrating that all peoples cry, laugh, eat, worry and die. It can introduce the idea that if we try and understand each other, we may even become friends.'

Maya Angelou

CHAPTER TWO

The Magical Land of Kenya

CHAPTER TWO
The Magical Land of Kenya

'The gladdest moment in human life, me thinks, is a departure into unknown lands.'

Sir Richard Francis Burton

Kenya is a country in East Africa, bordering the Indian Ocean in the South East; its neighbouring countries are Ethiopia, Somalia, South Sudan, Tanzania and Uganda. With an area of 580,000 km, the country is somewhat larger than or slightly bigger than the size of the US state of Nevada.

Now, let me introduce you to a few words in our language. *Jambo* means 'hello' and *hakuna matata* means 'no worries' and are the most commonly known words, at least by every person who lands in Kenya. The country is full of friendly people.

I was born in a rural area part of Tiribe in Kwale, in the former Coast Province of Mombasa. I remember when I was young, despite all the hard physical work I had to do, I lived with my grandmother in a four bedroomed house. My father was a well-respected man in my hometown, known for his good heart, who always liked to help others when he could, including helping a lot of young men to get employment.

Tiribe is on the outside of the Kwale district in the countryside, and the town is very green and fertile. If you drop any seeds on the ground they will sprout into healthy plants. At certain times of the year the elephants would arrive behind the houses and start eating the plantations. Although this is a natural occurrence, everyone had to be extra careful to not get attacked by the elephants. Being a small town, almost all the neighbours knew one

CHAPTER 2: The Magical Land of Kenya

another and that made it special. There was a sense of love and togetherness in the community and people were happy to help each other.

I lived there until I finished my primary school. That's when I left to start a new adventure in the big city of Nairobi.

The cultures in Kenya differ from district to district. The most commonly spoken languages are Swahili and English but there are 42 different languages spoken in Kenya, and most people can understand each other. In Mombasa there are nine closely related but distinctive peoples called the mijikenda. They are the Kauma, Chonyi, Jibana, Giriama, Kambe, Ribe, Rabai, Duruma, and Digo. My mum and dad come from the Digo clan. The members of each of the nine mijikenda groups speak a separate dialect of the same language. The language, Mijikenda, is one of the Northeast Coastal Bantu group of languages and is closely related linguistically and historically to other languages along the Kenyan and Tanzanian coasts.

The women in the coast province where I was born are always dressed in vibrant colours of African batik called *kanga*; this is the most common way of dressing. These women work hard to make sure there is life in the house. They are very good at multi-tasking: you will often see those who are carrying babies on their back, a bucket of water on their head and another gallon of water in their hands. To them, this is normal, this is what they do best. Although it is a tough life, you will not see them complaining as this is what they are used to.

Despite the poverty and hunger in some of the communities, people are still living their life with the few things that they have. They are happy, and share what they have with one another. As the saying goes, *hakuna matata,* or 'no worries'. I remember in the community where I used to live, people would borrow anything from their neighbours - this spirit of togetherness is very normal.

Being the second largest city after Nairobi, Mombasa offers travellers an exotic taste of the African tropics steeped in centuries of seafaring history. This cosmopolitan tourist hub is a paradise with its beauty from the north coast and, if you love a little exploration, jumping on the famous ferries of Likoni can be a memorable experience too and you will be amazed by the white beaches of the southern part of the city.

Let me give you a brief tour of the country cities and their beauty. Fort Jesus was built in 1593-1596 by the Portuguese, and is one of the historical places in Mombasa. Haller Park is for the animal lovers. In 1971 Dr Rene Haller transformed the abandoned limestone quarries in the area into a thriving nature reserve. Mombasa Marine National Park is one of the busiest of Kenya's offshore reserves, protecting the mangroves, seagrass beds, sandy beaches and coral reefs.

The North Coast beaches are a little livelier than the South Coast and the resorts are closer to the airport and Mombasa city. The old town is on the Southeast side of Mombasa Island, and is a reminder of the days when the Portuguese ruled this important port. The South Coast beaches are a world of natural beauty: turquoise seas lap sun-bleached beaches where tourists sprawl under rustling palms. The Mombasa Tusks are a famous landmark in the city. They were built to commemorate Queen Elizabeth's visit to Mombasa in 1952.

Mombasa is a major trade centre and home to Kenya's only large seaport, the Kilindini Harbour. Kilindini is an old Swahili term meaning 'deep'. The port is so-called because the harbour channel is naturally very deep. Other local industry includes the oil refinery with a capacity of 80,000 barrels a day. These two main industries have created massive job opportunities for the locals, as has the tourism industry.

The capital, Nairobi, is a magical city. From having the gorgeous Mt Kenya not far away, to owning a national park in the city, the land is fertile, the

CHAPTER 2: The Magical Land of Kenya

vegetation is green and there is abundant fresh air.

The most famous national park in Kenya is the Maasai Mara. It is named in honour of the Maasai people. It is globally famous for its exceptional population of Masai lions, African leopards and Tanzanian cheetahs, and the annual migration of the zebra, Thomson's Gazelle, and wildebeest to and from the Serengeti every year between July and October, known as the 'Great Migration'. This wild beast migration is a phenomenal tourist attraction, and even just watching it on television is stunning.

Further to the west is Kisumu, which is the third largest city in Kenya. The city has a shoreline on Lake Victoria, occupying the northern, western and part of the southern shores of the Winam Gulf.

RISING FROM THE DUST

CHAPTER THREE

My Teenage Years

'It's never too late to have a happy childhood. But the second one is up to you and no one else.'

Regina Brett's 45 Life Lessons

CHAPTER THREE
My Teenage Years

One does not easily heal from trauma. The scars will be visible for a long time, be they physical or emotional, but how you handle what happens to you is the most important thing. No one can make you heal and the healing process starts with you.

You must reconnect with the sacred place in yourself that was never traumatized or broken, never damaged in the first place: your true self, the innocent baby within you who is lovable and free.

Happiness is not a destination. Nor is it based on material things. Happiness is a state of mind. It is you, a choice that you have to make. It is about knowing yourself as pure and understanding that you are alive and that God has a purpose for your life. It is only when we realise that our problems are not permanent that we can live without self-judgement.

We must understand that no matter what life throws at us, in the end it will pass. Challenges pass - they always pass - and you remain. You are not broken: you are unbreakable.

My teenage years were full of darkness. I did not know much about life when growing up. I did not love the person I saw in the mirror. I was searching for myself, as the girl I saw in the mirror did not reflect who I was supposed to be.

I was fighting with everything within myself. I remember there was a moment I wished I could sleep and never wake up. I was unhappy because of the beatings, and I was becoming more and more aware that I did not have a mum and dad who really took care of me. I did not understand myself and nothing made any sense in life, either, as the only thing I saw each time I looked in the mirror was an ugly girl who was full of anger with herself and her life. I was ready to go, as I didn't want to hurt anyone. It was a battle I was fighting emotionally, and because I did not have anyone to talk to. I used to keep all my emotions to myself.

At the age of fifteen years, I finished primary school. That's when I moved from the countryside to live with my step mum in Nairobi. I remember very well she came to collect me from the countryside where I was living with my grandmother. At that time she already had two daughters.

My life in the big city started as I was waiting for my results before I could join high school. I wanted to feel part of the family, but it was unfortunate that my stepsisters were aware that we were not from the same mum and only shared the same blood from my dad. When they mentioned that to me I felt sad and left out, as I had always felt that we were one.

It is during this time that I met my best friend Bernice who was our neighbour. I consider myself very fortunate to have connected with her. I was very introverted, or self-conscious, based on my life encounters. But I had a good connection with Bernice: we liked each other, and she was lovable and understanding. Because I felt comfortable around her, I started opening up and sharing my stories with her. She would encourage me to be strong and not to punish myself, and told me that someday things would be different. My story was different to hers as she comes from a family who are connected to each other. They are all lovable people and ever since I met her I have felt a part of her family. I remember there were moments when I did not have sanitary towels and she would give me some of hers, that's how deep the friendship was. I will always be grateful to her that she was and still is a true friend.

In my childhood I had to learn to protect my feelings, but it was not easy sometimes as my stepsisters would ask me why I was living with them. They

CHAPTER 3: My Teenage Years

made it clear that I was not part of the family. I am truly grateful that I always had a place to call home despite the fact that I had the feeling that I was not appreciated. I think my father loved me dearly, although African parents never tell their children they love them, even when they do. The words 'I love you' are not common, at least not from where I come from. Parents never say 'I love you' to their children, or maybe I'm just not aware of the situation in other African families. Although my father never said he loved me, I always believed that he did, since he took care of me by making sure I had food and shelter, and also by taking me away from my mum's mother. I went to school and he paid for my school fees. He never stayed with his wife and kids due to the nature of his work as he was stationed away from the city where my step mother lived and worked. He used to come every weekend to visit but still I could not share what was going on in my life with him.

After a few months, the exam results were out and it was time for me to join high school. I was an average student and this was a big disappointment to my dad as he had hoped I would get good grades. It is normal for parents to have expectations, and sometimes when children don't meet these expectations parents can be disappointed, which can cause frustration. It was not possible for me to get in the best schools in Kenya because of my low grades, but my father managed to get me in a private school in Athi River. It was a girls' boarding school and it was 29 kilometres from Nairobi city centre, in the district of Machakos in the Eastern part of Kenya.

My father made it possible for me to join this boarding school, and my new life began. Everything was new to me, and the beginning of boarding school was not easy. I was far away from people that I knew, and the whole experience was not so much different with my own childhood experiences having to live in different homes, where I had had to live in a new place and connect with new people and new structures.

I knew with time I would find my way and form new bonds with the other girls in the school. Being in a boarding school was not easy but I enjoyed my time. I remember waking up every early morning to get ready for the morning studies, taking cold showers at 5:30 am, rushing to the kitchen to get a mug of porridge - the day started just like that. It became part of my routine, and in a way I enjoyed being there. Being in a boarding school, life can be hard sometimes, something that I did not know before I started. There were times the senior girls would molest the new form one student, calling to us 'hey, you form one!' just for their own fun. They felt that they were superior and that they had power over us, asking us to clean their bed spaces, do their laundry or even get their food from the cafeteria, but all this became part of my boarding school life.

In time boarding school became a second home for me. I got used to all the new challenges and began to focus on my studies. I realised the very reason for me being in school was to study, although academically I was struggling. I was scared I was not smart enough, and I did not want to fail and disappoint my father, so for this reason I studied very hard.

I knew if I fervently pushed myself I might succeed with my studies, because, as the saying goes, 'education is the key to success'. I knew that I wasn't in school to be someone else's servant, and slowly I began to stand up for myself and learn to say no to the senior girls when they asked me to do something for them. Although at first they would not take no for an answer, in time they learned to respect me.

I always looked forward to the end of term so I could go back home to my stepmother and her children, although the word 'home' was perhaps not the most appropriate word to describe it. I looked forward to going home as I was excited to tell them about my life at boarding school, but when I got home no one was excited to see me, which was very disappointing.

I moved on with boarding school life and before I started my second year my father transferred me to a new boarding school in the eastern part of Kenya where I stayed until I finished my fourth high school year. I had to start a new

CHAPTER 3: My Teenage Years

life, bond with the other girls and learn to find my way again. I met friendly people during my high school days and I still have contact with some of the girls from my school.

The routine at my new school was not different from my previous school. Although each school has different rules and regulations, most of the routines were similar. I was an average student but I was actively involved in some of the school activities. I played basketball and netball and was the best athlete in the school. I would get excited during athletics competitions, especially when my school won the competition. We won some trophies for the school, which I am sure are still at my school for display. I was also involved in acting classes and reciting poems. Our school even made it to the national level in drama, where we met most of the schools from around Kenya. It was a great experience, interacting with different people. That's where my strength was. I absolutely loved it and I could do it again.

Before I knew it, I was done with boarding school. I had not known that four years would go by so quick. I finished high school and there I was waiting for the final results.

'Look for something positive in each day, even if some days you have to look a little harder. Let the challenges make you stronger.'

Unknown

It is said that in every situation we should look for the advantages, even when it's not in our favour. I remember very well after I finished high school and was waiting for my results, another challenge confronted me. I had nowhere to stay so my dad sent me back to my grandmother's place to stay until the results were out. I found this to be very discouraging, having to start life in the countryside yet again, just as most of the children with whom I grew up had already left for the city.

That was difficult for me. I had been away for four years and I had to start a new life again, but this time as a nineteen year old adult. Although nothing had changed at my grandmother's home since I'd been gone, I had changed. After all the exposure to a big city and to connecting with different minds while at boarding school, I felt like I had been displaced.

What I realised is that I was thinking differently to most of my friends in the village because they had not been exposed to the experiences I had. Having to live with my grandmother was not a new thing as she had raised me, and my life was much the same, with me continuing to do daily what girls do in a household. At first it was okay, but with time I started getting bored with the same routine day in day out. As much as I wanted to do something to develop myself, there was nothing in the neighbourhood that I could get involved in. It felt like the longest time for me to have to wait to for my results, but as there was nothing I could do about it I had to learn to be patient.

A couple of months later my secondary results were out and I started to wonder if I would have the chance to go to college. Where I was living there was no college, so I started asking my dad what the game plan was. I remember he said, 'When I get a place for you to stay, then you might start college.'

He kept his word. He got me a place to stay with a cousin so that I could start. Some months later I returned to Nairobi, feeling lucky that my cousin agreed to shelter me so that I could start college. She did not even mind sharing her room with me, which I will always be grateful for. While I was staying with my cousin my father supported me with food and paid my school fees, but although I had food and shelter there was no enough money for my bus fare so I had to walk each day to and from college. I absolutely did not mind walking each day, even when it was raining and hard to walk. I didn't mind as I was grateful that I had a chance to step foot in a college, which is something that I had been hoping and praying for.

CHAPTER FOUR

The Power of Discovering

"When you are grateful fear disappears and abundance appears."

Anthony Robbins

CHAPTER FOUR
The Power of Discovering

I had lived up until that point believing that I was not smart. I don't remember being told that I was by the people I lived with, and it became a part of my inner belief. I don't remember having been praised for anything in my childhood, only being criticized, and this was very demotivating.

But I rediscovered my love of learning when I entered college to study Hotel Management. I went from being a D student at school to a B student who passed her exams. The difference was I was able to choose my own course. At last, I was learning about something that interested me. My learning was not just for a career or future income. I was following my passion and I was finding my voice and strength.

Having been able to join college made me so grateful. I knew if I studied hard and believed in the Divine Providence, I could make it and due to the fact that I had chosen a course that I loved, I knew things would be somehow different.

My college moments were never dull. I met good people who were nice and with whom I formed study groups. I was very fortunate to have a good teacher, who not only helped us to find out our own uniqueness, but who also guided us in the fundamentals of hotel management, in life after college and with how to get employment. He made me understand that there is more to life than only passing exams.

This is something that I never had in my high school time and perhaps that's why I struggled with my studies. We need to be surrounded by people who can motivate us! I look at it as having a fairy godmother, someone who supports us in our learning journey, and it can be a good classmate, a friend, a schoolteacher or, if you are in luck, your own parents. We each need someone who can remind us that we can achieve what we want to do. In my case I was lucky to have a good teacher who knew my strengths and weaknesses and helped me in the areas I needed help most.

We focused on the areas that I needed to succeed in my studies. Although I had to walk daily to college, I enjoyed it because I loved studying and I felt good about myself and no longer thought of how unintelligent I was. The two years went by so quickly and before I realised it, I was done with college.

I am very grateful to my father who took care of me in his own way, even though there was a lot of financial pressure on him. He was constantly reminded that I was not his only child and that he should save up some money for my other half brothers and sisters. Given that they believed I was not intelligent enough for college, they thought he was wasting his money on my college education. This reminds me of the quote from Brene Brown:

'It is not the critic who counts, not the man who points out how the strong man stumbles, or where the doer of deeds could have done them better. The credit belongs to the man who is actually in the arena, whose face is marred by dust and sweat and blood, who strives valiantly, who errs, and who comes short again and again, because there is no effort without error and shortcoming, but who does actually strives to do the deeds, who knows great enthusiasm, the great devotion, who spends himself in a worthy cause, who at the best knows in the end the triumph of high achievement, and who at the worst, if fails, at least fails while daring greatly.'

Brene Brown

CHAPTER 4: The Power of Discovering

Being my father's first born child, the pressure was always on me. I remember being reminded that my half siblings looked up to me and so I should be a good example. It was tough, as I always believed that each of us is created with our own flaws, own strengths and our own powers that cannot be compared with another person's. Even our own fingers are not alike, and the reason for each person's existence on this earth is different.

So once again I had to suppress my own feelings because of the pressure that was always on me. I didn't want to disappoint anyone, but what I have since realised is that I did not let my inner child blossom. I was afraid of failing, because failure was unacceptable. I knew I had disappointed my father by not being the daughter he had expected, and being a parent myself now, I have come to realise that parents expect a lot from their children, which can have such a huge impact on a child's development.

As a parent now I realise that my expectations may not suit my son, Jasper. We are all unique and have different strengths, and instead of pushing our children we need to love and support them in their development and praise the areas that they are good at. The goal is not to be the smartest but to do your best with your capability. By doing our best, we can, however, put ourselves in the best place for the next moment.

Sometimes the community will have an impact in our lives. Living up to community expectations can really be tough, but we learn from these experiences to become better citizens.

When one is criticized and disempowered most of the time, he or she develops a sense of not belonging. This can create low self-esteem and anxiety. As the saying goes, it's not how hard we fall but how quickly we get up.

We must also recognize our mistakes and learn from them because to repeat the same pattern is to play the fool. It is our responsibility to choose what works for us, no matter what someone else thinks. It is okay to follow orders but if it doesn't work or suit you I strongly believe choosing your own authentic path is a good thing.

It is okay to be you. As Louise Hay says, 'don't be afraid to be you. The world needs your unique brand of awesomeness.' However, living in a community where you are constantly reminded of where you come from can have a negative impact on a person. I started thinking that I was less of human because I had so many flaws and was so much less than I was supposed to be. I started believing I was stupid just because I didn't make it to university and didn't get the best grades in high school. But the fact is that we all learn in different ways and some of the best minds in history have never been to university or are high school dropouts. What matters is what you choose to do with your life.

I was very naïve, insecure and lacking in confidence as a young girl. I had my own dreams but, due to the pressure around me, I started being somebody else instead of being my authentic self.

'To reach our goals, we have to continually stretch ourselves and train our minds to look outside the box. It is true that we are our only problem and only solution... this means, we must train our minds to see the opportunities that are always waiting for us.'

Unknown

When I finished my college education I immediately started searching for work as I needed to start to fully take care of myself. I remember walking in the city of Nairobi, dropping my CV in to restaurants and hotels. It really did not matter to me what the position was: all I needed was work. I waited and waited. I prayed and I believed that an opportunity would come, but it felt like the longest time for me: a couple of months waiting and hoping

CHAPTER 4: The Power of Discovering

that things would fall into place. I was called in for interviews but I did not succeed in being offered the jobs. I felt disappointed with myself and I started going back to my old way of thinking that I was not intelligent.

I realise now that it is true that you become what you think, and that we ourselves are our only problem and our only solution. Although I had the qualifications for the jobs I applied for, I did not believe in myself and my strength. Because I had lived my entire life in fear and with no self-confidence, I doubted my capabilities and perhaps that could be the reason I did not get any of the jobs I had applied for.

I remember asking myself: what is my next move? Yes, I had to choose whether to accept the situation or look for something else to do.

'For everything that has happened to you, you can either feel sorry or treat what has happened as a gift.
Everything is either an opportunity to grow or an obstacle to keep you from growing, you get to choose.'

Dr Wayne Dyer

In order for us to succeed we must push ourselves to be able to take other decisions. The reality is we all do know what we want for ourselves. If we keep on worrying and asking why the things that were so important in our life have turned into dust, our attitude will cause limitations in our life, and we will not only block ourselves from receiving our blessings, but will also cause stress for everyone who is involved.

There are certain challenges in life that we may not be able to avoid: no one knows what might happen in a day. Things pass and the best we can do is to let them go. That is why no matter how painful it is, sometimes we have to move on. Everything in this world that happens is based on our way of thinking and the limitations we create for ourselves, and when we learn to let go we are creating room for new things.

We all have the power to choose what we want to do with our lives. We can choose to be lesser people than God has created us to be, or we can strive for a better life. We get to choose.

My journey of searching for work did not stop. I found myself repeating the exact same process again, going around and delivering my CV to different workplaces in the hope of finding employment. But by this time I had learned my lesson, so I was very conscious of not repeating the same mistake of self-sabotage. I remember talking to my friend Bernice about finding a job and she said, 'What belongs to you will always come in your path.' I did not want to believe her words but a month later another opportunity came up and I went in for another interview. I remember walking in and there were two other girls who had come for the same interview. I walked out of the interview knowing that I had done my best. They had asked me to step out of the room and that they would call me in after deliberation.

I started telling myself I could not have done better than that. I prayed and I believed that the position was mine. After thirty minutes of waiting I was called in. I was shaking, my heart was pounding, the fear started to creep in again, but I had to wait for their answer. I was asked to sit down and I remember they asked me, 'When would you like to start?'

I did not know how to feel. I started believing that my prayers had been answered and I became very emotional. My answer was 'thank you for believing in me for the job, can I start tomorrow please?'

My new employers said 'yes, if you are ready.'

CHAPTER 4: The Power of Discovering

I thanked them and I walked out of the room and off I went. As I was walking to the bus stop, I felt like a little child who had been given a candy. I was very happy. I thanked the Creator for making these dreams a reality, and I went home feeling like I had achieved something huge. A dream had come true. I had a job.

'It's the possibility of having a dream come true that makes life interesting.'

Paulo Coelho

CHAPTER FIVE

Becoming Truly Independent

CHAPTER FIVE
Becoming Truly Independent

And so a new chapter in my life began. I remember waking up one morning realizing that I had achieved something. I had a job, arranged totally by myself, and I could now start taking care of myself fully.

I met nice colleagues who were willing to train me in my new role. I enjoyed working, although working on shifts was quite tiring sometimes. What kept me going was the idea of being independent. I started feeling in charge of my life for the very first time. I knew the future would be beautiful, or at least I had a new hope for a bright future. I started believing that my life would slowly start to change now that I had a job and could start taking care of myself.

'When we least expect it, life sets us a challenge to test our courage and willingness to change; at such moment, there is no point in pretending that nothing has happened or saying that we are not yet ready. The challenge will not wait. Life does not look back. A week is more than enough time for us to decide whether or not to accept.'

Paulo Coelho

While I was in the midst of celebrating having a new job I learned that I could not stay any longer with my cousin as she needed to start her own family, and there was not enough space to accommodate everyone. I will always be grateful for her having sheltered me while I was in college, but the news came to me unexpectedly just as I started working and had not saved any money yet. I became depressed, and could not understand why my life

CHAPTER 5: Becoming Truly Independent

was full of bad luck. At that moment I could not yet afford a small home for myself, and I needed to come up with a solution. I remember informing my father of what was happening, and he asked me to go back home to where he was living. For the first time I had the chance to live with my father. Life started to unfold for me. I had a job and at last I was living back at home.

Based on the nature of my job I sometimes had to work late shifts, getting home after midnight and getting up for the morning shift the next day. In the kind of customer service role I had we had to work shifts, which is quite normal in the service industry. But this brought a lot of doubt to my father and his family. They could not understand why I would work until so late and start so early the next day. People thought I worked during the daytime and did different things at night; they even called me a prostitute, thinking I did other business in the evening. Again people judged me quickly, without knowing the facts. This was so hard for me. Those who have worked in the hotel or other service industries know how it is to work shifts. I felt heartbroken and I started going back to my old way of thinking, that I am less than other people and not loved. Although it was hard to take it, I had to live with my sorrows. I did not have any energy for my work anymore, but I needed to do it so that I could have my own financial freedom.

After I worked for a couple of months, my father asked me to find a place of my own because I was working now and I was an independent girl. This simple message from my father came to me as a big shock. How was it possible that my own father would just put me out of the house without asking if I earned enough to take care of myself and rent a property on my own?

I did not have a lot of money. I remember I had 40,000 Kenyan shillings in savings and that was not a lot of money to start afresh. But, as the message from my father was clear and firm, I needed to come up with a plan as to how to put my life together with this amount of money. I spoke to my colleagues at work and they were willing to help me out to get a place. I started searching for a small house and luckily I got a studio apartment.

RISING FROM THE DUST

'Only when we are brave enough to explore the darkness will we discover the infinite power of our light.'

Unknown

I moved into my new home and started a new life with my job and my small room for myself. I was very conscious about budgeting for what I should buy for my little nest. My budget was very tight, so I had to opt for only the most important things, and I told myself the rest would come later when I have money. I was 22 years old and responsible for managing my life with the little income that I had. I knew I had to be extra careful in making my own decisions, and as much as it was a stressful time for me putting my life together, I started believing and having faith that all things work together for good. I accepted my fate day by day and with time I fully loved and enjoyed my new home.

In everything that happens in our life, no matter how hard things can be, I strongly believe there is a higher reason as to why things happen the way they do, and that is to teach us and make us stronger. We must be willing to know the hidden message. I believe God loves us dearly and when we have faith and hope, we find the courage to believe in what we cannot see and the strength to let go of our fear of uncertainty. It is only by believing and having faith and hope that through all this confusion something good will come. I started praising myself for doing a great job of taking care of me and that's when I learned that gratitude unlocks the fullness of life. Gratitude turns what we have to being enough and turns denial into acceptance, chaos into clarity, problems into gifts, failures into successes, and the unexpected into perfect timing.

CHAPTER 5: Becoming Truly Independent

What we perceive as mistakes can turn into a blessing.

The work I was doing was good. I enjoyed the fact that I was financially independent, although it was a struggle to cope with the different shifts. After a while it became part of my life and I had energy to go for it with enthusiasm. I slowly started to save some money for the 'rainy' days. Based on the life that I have lived, I had to teach myself to be sensible. I knew if I kept some money aside, I would use it for buying more things that I needed for my house.

> *'The greatest pleasure in life is doing what people say you cannot do.'*
> Walter Bagehot

After putting my life together I decided to go back to college to do further studies. I decided to do a diploma in marketing and public relations. Since I had only a certificate in hotel management, I needed to develop myself. An investment in knowledge always pays the best interest and, as the saying goes, knowledge is power and no one can ever take it away from you. This was my motto that made me go back to college.

I had saved up some money so that I could pay for my college fees and this made me feel like I had become an independent woman, making decisions for myself. Juggling work and part-time studies was not easy but I kept on reminding myself that anything is possible if I put my mind in to it.

Although working and studying is never the easiest combination, I needed to discipline myself to set some rules for myself so that I could complete my studies. Also, when you know your 'why', that's what makes you to keep going. I needed to develop myself since I did not want to work in a hotel for the rest of my life. Although I was happy that I had a job and that I could take care of myself, I really felt like it was not what I wanted to do in the long term, even though I will always be grateful for having had that job. I learnt a lot by dealing with different customers but also by connecting with my colleagues. I knew I could change my career if I wanted to and that is the very reason that I made a drastic change and did Marketing and Public Relations. Two years later when I had finished my studies, I started looking for public relations work but I was never lucky enough to get to work with a PR organization. I was disappointed, but unfortunately we are living in a world where sometimes it is who you know that matters, and not what you have.

'If you live through defeat, you are not defeated. If you are beaten but acquire wisdom, you have won. Lose yourself to improve yourself. Only when we shed all self-definition do we find who we really are.'

Unknown

When we are born we do not think of inadequacies. Our minds are clear and full of positivity. We start thinking 'I cannot' as we grow, based on what we hear and see through the adults around us. I do not remember criticizing myself when I was a young girl. These feelings started when I became aware of what was happening around me. I did not know about sin until I heard I was born out of a sinful relationship. This made me hate myself even more. Most of our thoughts are primarily a glimpse of our self-judgements, self-criticism, doubt and so many other things that we pick up as we grow. I think that these thoughts do not come from self-love but rather from a self-image that believes in fear. We start looking at what is happening around us and believe just that. We start thinking that we are not good enough, unintelligent, or unlovable based on self-hate.

The world can be a dark and lonely place if we do not know who we are, do not love ourselves and we do not know the reason for our existence. We see things not as they are, but as we are. It is true that what we believe can

CHAPTER 5: Becoming Truly Independent

become a reality to ourselves. I suffered a disease called lack of self-love. I was raised by people who did not feel loveable, they never taught me how to love and hence I did not know how to love myself. Most African parents or adults will not tell you they love you, they will show affection but the words never come out. I used to mirror my problems to the world. I blamed the very fact of my existence. I had a lot of mixed feelings and I suffered from my own psychology. What I did not know was that life itself was not against me. The universe loves us but we need to be open to see it. Only when we do that, everything else falls in place.

It is very easy to fall in to being a victim, especially when we do not know the true essence of our being. We get lost in what is happening around us and forget the very reason for our existence. When I look back to my teenage years, I had no idea what the true meaning of life was. Everything was confusing. I had so many more questions than answers as to why I was created. I lived day by day, buried in a ditch of regrets. I had so many regrets as to my reasons of existence and I had no idea what I was living for. I felt that life did not love me, until I discovered that these were my own limited thoughts.

Feeling powerless

'The hardest part is when you can't do anything about it. When you know you want to and you know you would. If you could'

Unknown

We all have moments in our life that we crucify ourselves for whatever reason. When I look at myself, I know I have lived my life feeling a lot of guilt. The guilt problem is something that a lot of us can relate to. But each one of us has our own version of it, depending on what has happened in our life.

Guilt is caused by not feeling innocent. It is what we experience when we forget who we are. I lost my innocence because of who my family expected me to be versus who I was and this is the reason that I had so many regrets about all the things that I did. I wanted to be a good daughter, niece and granddaughter but because I had so much pain with what had been happening in my life, I lost sight of my innocence. Innocence is the true nature of us as humans. I was searching for love from my family which I believed was not there and that's perhaps why I was hurt. It's easy to identify ourselves with labels others have chosen for us, but we can also choose to love who we are no matter what. It took me many years before I knew and truly felt that what had happened between my mum and dad had nothing to do with me.

I now fully understand that feeling guilty never changes anything, but only destroys you emotionally.

'Fear binds the world. Forgiveness sets it free.'

Unknown

It is impossible to be happy and at the same live a fearful life. I had lived my life trying to be a good girl who was searching for love, but what I didn't know was that the more I tried to be a good girl, the more I had to pretend. I thought that if I suppressed my feelings and happiness I could be someone else and perhaps I could be loved. That was never the case. I traded my happiness for a pretence. I was searching for love and approval, and I took my childhood trauma into adulthood with me. In the long run I was lost because I was not being sincere to myself. What I did not know was that loving myself could help in forgiving my past and those who had wronged me, and could help me realise that I did my best at every stage of my life.

I was still judging myself for not have been the good little girl that I was expected to be by my family. I felt I had made many mistakes. I had failed my

CHAPTER 5: Becoming Truly Independent

father by not being the daughter he expected. But failing to forgive yourself will trap you in a prison of unworthiness. Forgiveness is the only way to release the past: when we forgive we set ourselves free.

Forgiveness is the simplest thing and yet the most difficult for a lot of people. The word 'forgive' sounds very powerful and mostly people find it hard to just do it, but I think it is caused by our ego. We think if we forgive then we are giving our power away to whoever has wronged us. But the reality is that it is only when we forgive that we can set ourselves free.

Forgiveness has nothing to do with the other person; it is to do mostly with ourselves. Only when we forgive we can set ourselves free from feeling guilt. I remember when I was called a prostitute because I was working shifts in a hotel. This made me feel like I had lost my identity and that's why I buried myself in a ditch of emotion and guilt. I felt unworthy due to others' mistaken perceptions of me. I didn't love myself because I did not see the reason to. I struggled with self-hatred until my friend Bernice said I had to let it go.

'Letting go?' I remember asking her. 'How do you let go of a mistaken perception?'

Her answer was it really did not matter what people say, because at the end of the day it is who you think you are that matters. My inner child was unhappy and I had to forgive myself for the mistaken perceptions of others.

I went through a period in my life where I had to ask myself who I was and what was the meaning of what was happening. In the midst of all this confusion I needed to understand how I'd get through it to the other side better than when I went in. I wanted to wake up each morning having peace within, and knowing that I had done my best.

RISING FROM THE DUST

When I look back at all the broken pieces in my life, and at all the baggage I acquired based on my limited thinking, what I learned is that we need to learn not to make the broken pieces look scary and big. When we wish to fix these pieces back together, sometimes we create more pain for ourselves. Instead, we need to come to a place in our life where we rise above all the labels we have been given by other people, and those false labels we have identified with. We must connect all the broken pieces, but in order for us to be able to do that we need to make it clear to the conscious mind that from all this confusion something good is going to come to us. What I have learned from my journey while I was trying to connect my broken pieces is that you must love and approve of who you are, despite all the circumstances around you, and when you love and approve of yourself, you deserve good. God loves us so dearly and life is just wonderful and will bring what we need even though we may not know we need it.

In every situation we encounter in our life it is very important that we realise how much power we have. We must not focus on the negative side of our problems. I have learnt that it is essential to be grateful for everything good, no matter how little it may be. So often we fail to appreciate the little things we have because we are busy looking at what others have. But if we love and are grateful for the little things we have, that's when we get to have more things in abundance.

> *'Devotion is the reverent, personal act of surrendering your will to Divine will. When we become devoted to healing our inner world, loving and honoring ourselves and using that love as the standard by which we interact with others, all the riches of this life will fall into our laps.'*
>
> Iyanla Vanzant

CHAPTER SIX

Choose Wisely

> *'Bad days build better days.'*
>
>
>
> Aubrey Nolan

CHAPTER SIX
Choose Wisely

In life there will be good days and bad days and we should be grateful for them all. Each day is a blessing, I have taught myself each morning to wake up with positive energy.

The first thing I do in the morning is to pray. I ask God to guide me and to take charge of all the activities that I am planning to do that day. I also pray for the things we do not plan for as human beings, as things can change any time and we might not have any power over them but when we ask the Divine Protector to be in charge we are surrendering our wishes to Him. It is important to count our blessings, to appreciate what we have. Gratitude opens the door for more blessings.

'Lives fall apart when the foundation upon which they were built needs to be re-laid.'

Iyanla Vanzant

It is human nature to question ourselves and, sometimes we ask God why certain things aren't the way we want. I, too, have had many questions about my relationship with my family, but I now understand that lives fall apart, not because God is punishing us for what we have or have not done. Lives fall apart because they need to. These things need to happen because the foundation isn't built the right way in the first place, especially if there is not much love in a relationship, which can cause a lot of friction. There are times when we do not recognize that it is time for us to move forward. When life is ready for us to move and we resist, life will move us by any means necessary. What may feel like a disaster can actually be a blessing. We must remain open to being guided, supported and protected by the Universe.

We are the only ones responsible for what goes on in our lives. We can make excuses and blame others, but we are responsible for ourselves. Most of us know exactly what it is that creates the pain, confusion, stagnation and disruption in our lives. We must muster the courage and strength to stop it.

Knowing who you are eliminates the guess-work in life. When you know who you are, you are open to every experience. You know there is always room for self-improvement and that where you are is an opportunity. You also need to forgive yourself for all of the unkind, unloving, unsupportive things you have thought about yourself. Forgive yourself for the things you have done to yourself, that support the things you believe about yourself that are not true. Forgive yourself for being so hard on yourself.

I have taught myself to be kind. I imagine that I am my own best friend, whispering positive and comforting words in my ear and letting go of the voices of self-doubt and self-criticism. I have learned to acknowledge and appreciate the 90% that I have achieved instead of the 10% that I didn't.

> *'Walk with the wise and become wise,*
> *for a companion of fools suffers harm.'*
>
> Proverbs 13:20

Choose your circle wisely

I did not have many friends when growing up, as I was ashamed of them knowing my personal life. Although I knew a lot of people, I never really invested in friendship as I used to think people wouldn't like me and might use the negative things about myself that I shared with them to hurt me. That is why I only had one friend who really understood me and that's Bernice.

CHAPTER 6: Choose Wisely

Bernice has been there for me, come rain or sunshine. But as I started loving and accepting myself I started creating new friendships. To me, friendship is love because we choose who we want to stick around with: we can't choose our families but we can choose our friends. What I did not know was that you can love your friends but don't expect the same from them, especially if they are only acquaintances.

There is a statement that says 'show me your friends and I will tell what kind of a person you are'. When I first heard this I challenged whoever stated it. I used to think that whatever our friends choose to do or say has nothing to do with us because we're totally different people. We are all responsible for our own choices and decisions, but I also think that we have the choice to choose our friends and with that said we can only choose the people who we feel comfortable to be around. Friends are people who should bring the brilliance out of us, and not drain us. We choose them because of the love we share with them, and the beauty of life. But sometimes friends can disappoint too. In my twenties I learnt that some friends can be a disgrace or even disappointing. I have learnt that it is very important to have an open mind about people so that you do not get hurt.

I have learned that there are four different kinds of people. There are those who do not like to share anything: the ones who discourage you and condemn your future plans. There are those who will not support you, but when you become successful they will be the first ones to undermine you, asking why you did it this way instead of that. It is unfortunate that it takes only a few people who actually can appreciate what other people are doing and as much as this can be frustrating it is very important that if you have anything in mind that you want to do to just get up and do it. Of course, you might have doubts and wonder what people will think. But what we should ask is: does it matter what they think? It really does not matter who praises you so long as it gives you pleasure. Then it's absolutely worth the risk.

But also there are the ones whom you might not see or talk to daily, but when you see them it feels good to be with them, they are genuine and their intention is to help you and see you happy. You can pick up a conversation from your last talk with them, and that's what friends are for. They don't judge you for being you: they uplift you, admire your strength and bring out the best in you. These are the friends we should stick around with. I have been lucky to have a few of these kinds of friends.

Friendship shouldn't be based on comparing ourselves with what another person has. It's not about material things, but about loving each other. I am so grateful to my childhood friend Bernice. She has been there for me in good and bad, and has never judged me for what was happening in my life. She supported me, encouraged me and stood by my side. I will always be grateful to have had her friendship since we were kids. It amazes me how both of us have grown to be individual confident women with our own families. Even though we don't see each other as often as we did before (as we now live in different parts of the world), one thing that I do know is that she will always be there for me.

It is so important to choose your circle very carefully, as these are the people you will most often be around and the last thing you need is to be drained. I am grateful to have met lovely ladies in my expat life and they are just fun to be around with. Always remember: never be afraid to let go of people who are only reflecting your negativity. Stay around those who support you, those who are genuinely happy to see you succeed. At the same time, people will leave your life because your energies do not attract each other anymore. That is fine, take those moments to love yourself. There is nothing to lose by just being you. We have to learn to let go of those who cannot support or celebrate our success. It is only when we do so that the universe connects us with positive and likeminded people.

CHAPTER 6: Choose Wisely

'Words can inspire. And words can destroy. Choose yours well.'

Robin Sharma

It was early in April 2015. I remember I was out with my little darling Jasper, having mummy and son bonding time. As usual, Jasper was playing Minecraft on my phone and a Facebook Messenger message came through. He passed the phone to me so I could read the message, and when I opened the message, the content shocked me to the core of my being. I was told that I was an embarrassment to my family for being me, for following my authenticity to find my purpose in life, and that God should punish me. I was told that if I didn't ask for forgiveness from above, then the day I died I would go to hell!

I was in shock. I looked at the text and asked myself: what is the lesson I should be learning from this? At that moment I was shaken, and my mood changed. I looked at the message again to see if I had read it correctly. I started wondering what I had done wrong to deserve such kind of pain. I wondered whether I should reply or not, before finally deleting it.

I have always taught myself since a young age, and based on my life challenges, that when someone does something bad to you - as much as it can be painful - never repay bad behaviour with bad action or words. We have a saying in my mother tongue that is delicately translated from Swahili to English that says 'when a mad person walks around in the city naked don't do the same, otherwise people will not know who is who'. Although I was hurt by the message, I did not want to reply with a mean message. I had the choice to do so, but I knew if I did, I would be giving my power away. I know God wants me to be me and that's why there is only one person who looks like me and that's me.

God loves us and He does not hate, condemn or punish us. People who are struggling with their own emotions will always try to reflect their problems to other people so that they feel good about themselves. And if you are not strong enough to stand your ground, you can easily be broken by what other people think about you. It is not our responsibility to make other people be nice and kind to us: when you know who you are, nothing else matters.

CHAPTER SEVEN

Acceptance and Forgiveness

'Adversity gives birth to greatness. The greater the challenges and difficulties we face, the greater the opportunity we have to grow and develop as people. A life without adversity, a life of ease and comfort, produces nothing and leaves us with nothing. This is one of the indisputable facts of life.'

Daisaku Ikeda

CHAPTER 7: Acceptance and Forgiveness

CHAPTER SEVEN
Acceptance and Forgiveness

When we humans are in the midst of a problem, the only focus we normally have is on the problem of what is happening. We close our minds, we don't see the light anymore, and we block the positive energy because our focus is only on the issues we are dealing with. There is nothing in this life that is permanent. All of our experiences, no matter how difficult they seem to be, are just temporary. However, it is not easy to accept this and just let things go, especially if you are in the middle of a bad experience. In order for us to free ourselves from the bad experience we are facing, we need to force ourselves to look at the circumstances we are in and try to look for the truth of what is happening. No matter how strong we are in our faith, challenges will always be there but no matter what happens we must not doubt our faith.

When I look back at my younger self, I had such a heavy heart full of pain. I used to feel miserable and always had the feeling that I was the problem. I didn't know how to deal with my pain. It was not easy to just accept and let it go as we are taught, but what I have learnt as a mature adult now is that I have the power to reshape and redefine any experience, no matter how devastating it seems. Sometimes we need to be hurt in order to grow, we must lose in order to gain, and sometimes lessons are learned through pain. I have learned to look at any experience and ask myself how I can use it for my own growth. It is by doing so that we heal ourselves. Acceptance of an experience as being temporary can make it a lot easier to manage. Fighting back sometimes means giving away your power and that's what the enemy wants: to make you feel sorry for yourself. But if you let go, the universe will help you with the healing process.

'Do not let anything from your past inhibit you in this present moment. Start over. Start fresh. Each day. Each hour, if it serves you. Heck, each minute. Just get going. Just do it. Just say it. With love. All else will take care of itself.'

Neale Donald Walsch

When we choose to accept ourselves and our lives as they are, and when we accept that the person we used to be is dead and buried, we are making our conscious mind clear. This is the way we start to embrace who we are. It is only when we get to this level of clarity about who we are and are not, as well as who we are choosing to be, that we get a different response to what we truly want for ourselves.

It is our responsibility to know who we are in order to embrace life fully. Knowing who we are can make us live our lives fully, with self-love and without guilt. If we spend our whole lives trying to be who everyone else expects us to be, we are running away from being our authentic selves.

I have been given all sorts of labels, and told that I will never make it in life. I was once told that if I was not careful I would die of HIV. And I used to believe those things I was told, because I had not yet encountered the real Fauza. In African culture, when somebody is insulted with the word 'prostitute' it's a very big insult. It's meant to bring the other person down. These words still rotate in my mind, like when you are playing music and press the 'repeat' button: this is how it feels sometimes when I am alone and I start meditating on my life.

Growing up as a female child who never knew what it is to be loved is all I knew. It can hurt when you live a life of knowing that you are not appreciated. I used to feel like there was no meaning to life, but it is through my triumphs that I became strong and started fighting life and its challenges. Sometimes when I look back on everything I've been through, it makes me even stronger.

CHAPTER 7: Acceptance and Forgiveness

It's unfortunate that so often we silence our inner voices because we are afraid of being judged. But for how long will you live a life of pleasing others while on the other hand you are hurting yourself?

When I was growing up with my granny in the country, I used to see the family elders taking charge of things and making the decisions. This is considered to be normal in the culture. It is unfortunately the case, however, that even today there are still people living a 19th century life in my village. When you are born a girl, you do not have the power to speak for yourself, and any major decisions are made on your behalf. It's a shame because we are all created with our own power, and we are all unique. But if you are struggling and searching for your identity, at times it can be hard. I didn't know this until I read the book *You Can Heal Your Life* by Louise Hay. It is after reading her story that I felt the connection and started thinking it really doesn't matter how people look at me or how they call me because I now know WHO I AM. When I look back everything makes me even stronger.

'It's not enough to simply claim that you care about yourself; when you believe that you're worthy of the space you occupy on the planet, you demonstrate that by insisting that every last one of your choices - from the food you put in your mouth to the commitments you put on your calendar - moves you toward the life you want.'

Oprah Winfrey

The core values of my life are built around one thing only and that is believing and having hope that, no matter what happens, God will never abandon His own children. He has given us the power to be all that we can be through His guidance. I strongly believe He has been guiding me through my journey. Otherwise, I wouldn't have written this book you are reading. We need to have courage over fear. I always look at my life and ask what it is that is so important for me. When you have found the answer to this question everything else will fall into place. Because when we take charge of what is really important in our lives, we focus all the positive energy in that area. It's about being deliberate, conscious and aware of the choices that we make every day that adds up to living the life that we want to create.

I believe wholeheartedly that each one of us has a purpose but I know from firsthand experience that awakening to it requires us to tell ourselves some rough, rugged and raw truths to get really clear about the life that we want to be leading.

It is easy to just sit back and blame all the circumstances we encounter, but if we do nothing, nothing is going to change. No one is responsible for our life. We are the only ones who are in charge of what we truly want, and if we realise this, all the confusions of this life becomes clear in our mind. We must be the change we want to see in our lives.

I know for myself, I used to blame everything that was happening but I never changed the situation until I stopped complaining about my problems and started being in charge. That's when my life started to unfold. Before that everything was dark and I was stuck. I decided to live my life with a purpose and enthusiasm that gives me energy in every area of my life. I check my choices against who I say I am versus who I want to be. I often ask myself if I am being intentional about creating a life and not just sitting back and expecting life to happen for me. Am I allowing myself to be expanded by life, or am I running away from all the challenges that I encounter? Do my actions line up with who I say I am or want to be? Are my values rooted in soul-based goals that connect me to how I want to feel on a daily basis, versus the superficial ones that I think will make me feel good?

CHAPTER 7: Acceptance and Forgiveness

It is very easy to just sit back and wait for things to happen but what I have learnt is that no matter how many times we pray, prayer without taking action is not going to change anything in our life. We are the only ones who can create the change that we want to see. I remember a couple of years back when I was really depressed and confused with myself. I would pray and once I was done I would go back in my comfort zone and re-think of the same problems over and over again and nothing was changing in my life. The problems that I had did not change; instead, things were getting worse, because I was only concentrating on what was happening around me until I started focusing on the positive things about life.

Even being alive is a massive blessing. I told my inner baby to stop feeling sorry for herself about what has happened in the past, and to move on. It is easy to just sit and do nothing but at the end of the day we are the ones to take charge of our lives, and no matter how difficult it is, we need to move on. It is only by doing so that we start to live life fully.

'You can't connect the dots by looking forward; you can only connect them by looking backwards. So you have to trust that the dots will somehow connect in your future. You have to trust in something - your gut, destiny, karma or whatever.'

Steve Jobs

I remember when I was growing up, I was never allowed to visit my mother. I never understood why but when you are a child sometimes there are things that are decided for you and you just have to accept the situation and move on. I was once told that if I was not careful I would be like my mother who had kids from different relationships. This made me have a lot of questions with no answers. It is only when I was an adult and wanted to reconnect and start a new bond with my mother again that I began to understand a little more of myself from her side of the story.

At a very young age I was angry with my mother about her not taking care of me instead of my grandmother. After many conversations between us, and after she explained to me her own circumstances, then everything made sense to me. I want to think every woman would want to see their child grow if they possible can. Sometimes women are not able to raise their children due to the circumstances of their lives, and sometimes they are forced to leave their children to be taken care of by relatives. When I look at myself as an adult woman, I understand how painful it can be for a mother not to be able to raise her own child. Although I had so many questions for my mother when I was a young adult, I am now in a position to accept that I will not get all the answers. I now understand that what happened was not fully under her control. No woman chooses not to raise her children, unless there are unavoidable circumstances.

My mother is a very beautiful woman; she loves to smile and has a kind heart, although she is not outspoken, she is a lovely woman to be around. Although my relationship with her is different based on our past life, one thing that I know is that she did what she did based on the circumstances around her. At least, this is what she said to me.

'I forgive everyone in my past for all perceived wrongs. I release them with love.'

Louise Hay, *Forgiving and Letting Go*

CHAPTER 7: Acceptance and Forgiveness

Forgiveness is the beginning of healing ourselves. If we don't forgive ourselves for everything that we have done, we are not going to be able to forgive others for what they have done to us. Forgiveness was the hardest thing for me to do. I never saw any reason as to why I should forgive someone for hurting me. It took me many years before I could really learn to forgive. This was after a lot of talks with myself. I was very bitter and angry about all that had happened in my life.

I never understood why the people who should have been there for me were the ones cursing me. I had to teach myself to forgive because that is the only way to have peace within. I knew when I let go of my uncertainty I could be happy with who I am. I forgive all those who have hurt me. I forgive myself for hurting others. I forgive myself for blaming and punishing myself. I forgive myself for hurting my parents. I forgive my parents for hurting me.

Forgiveness is a gift to ourselves. We need to learn to forgive in order to free ourselves from our past experiences. When we forgive we allow ourselves to live in the present moment. When we forgive ourselves and others we create peace for ourselves, but we also acknowledge our past experiences. It does not necessarily mean that we condone the behaviour of those who have wronged us, but we must be able to forgive from our heart. By setting ourselves free from holding on to the pain that was caused to us, we release ourselves from the negative energy.

It took me a lot of years to really mean what I say and the day I meant my forgiveness I felt very light. I was set free from my bondage of pain and anger, and slowly there was a difference within me, and I was a little happier too.

When we find our own authentic self, it is a beautiful thing knowing that the powerful essence of the creator is there to guide and lead us. When we love ourselves without judgement, without societal prejudice, without expectation, that's when we find peace within. When we know who we are, accept why we are and understand our purpose in life, we can come to a self-realization that becomes a constant source of encouragement. Loving yourself enough to rise above the old experiences is the best gift that a person can give himself or herself.

Forgiving has nothing to do with changing your past. When you set yourself free you become aware of your own power. It has taken me a great deal of time to fully understand that forgiveness is the simplest yet hardest thing to do, but in order for us to live a life with no regrets, no pain and no blame we must dive deep down inside our hearts to seek our own healing. It might be hard when we do it at first, but as we practise daily to let go, in time we become aware of our feelings and that's when the magic starts to unfold: we start to become happy, the baggage on our back slowly becomes lighter, and as time goes by we slowly begin to heal, accept our situations and even love ourselves a little more. I have learned to let things go. I have taught myself that what I cannot influence or change I must release with love. I choose not to give my power away, to love myself a little more and accept who I am fully.

CHAPTER EIGHT

Searching for One's Happiness

'The path to happiness is rarely a straight line but, there are so many opportunities for wisdom along the way.'

Oprah Winfrey

CHAPTER EIGHT
Searching for One's Happiness

Sometimes I think life is like driving on a road with no streets lights. We rely on the car's headlights. We don't see the whole road ahead of us, but we never stop driving. We keep on going and as we go along we are able to see the next part of the journey.

If we are scared to make choices in our lives, we are going to be stuck and never progress. It is only when we trust in ourselves and the universe that we deserve something good that becomes easier to make any progress in our life.

When I was struggling with myself and my life, I remember saying often to myself, 'one day, everything that has happened in my life will have been a worthy experience.' But in order for me to move on in my life I needed to understand what I was supposed to do with my life and how I could change my life to make things better.

The transformation of the way you look at your life is a lifelong process. Rome was not built in one day. At least it wasn't for me, and I still have days when the sky is dark and gloomy. But you can change, no matter how desperate or unspeakable your circumstances are.

I lived for so many years not knowing who I was, because of what had been said about me.

It was not easy to accept some things. Sometimes we are supposed to accept so that we can move on. I used to ask myself how I could accept the things that I was falsely accused of. There were moments I wished that I had not been born, or I wished I could die so that I was no longer in this world. I wasn't happy with myself.

RISING FROM THE DUST

It has taken me many years to accept myself fully. I have learnt that as long as you are in this world people will call you names, but it is how you respond that will make the difference.

I never loved myself because I never felt that I was loved. When I was growing up I never knew what the meaning of love was. I eventually decided to look for a professional help, and I poured my heart out to my counsellor, but the only solution I could find was to accept and love myself. My counsellor told me if I could learn to let go of what has been said about me, I could embrace the real me. She told me that it is not about the labels that I had been given, but about who I believed I was that truly matters.

I have learnt that I am unique and I am a strong woman because it really doesn't matter what people think of you. It's not relevant what they call you, what matters is what you call yourself.

People will always make assumptions, they will call you names but if you know who you are, you can stand up to it and for yourself, because there is only one you and you are unique.

I remember when I took my first tiny, shaky steps away from the depression and anxiety that consumed me. It was a huge struggle, I kept on moving back and forth, but as I look over my shoulder now, the anxiety and depression no longer bears down on me, waiting to pounce. There is enough distance between them and the road that I am on now for me to look to the future, rather than the past. There are moments when I find myself thinking about how I got from there to here, and feeling immensely grateful for that journey. When my world imploded I had no idea just how many steps it would take to find and stay on the right path that would lead me out my darkness and back to the light. There were plenty of proverbial 'one step forward and two steps back' moments, and more than once I wanted to leave the path altogether. But I managed to cobble together a roadmap of sorts that helped to guide me. Everyone's journey is different and unique as is his or her recovery.

CHAPTER 8: Searching for One's Happiness

Forgiveness gave me a chance to be Fauza and be the real me.

'When you have confidence in your own path, you can make your own choices in religion or love.'

Fauza Beltz

The first relationship with my parents is the first mirror in my life. There is no doubt that my body was created from their bodies; they gave me my name Fauza, which means victorious, triumphant, successful, and their religion is also mine by birth. My first language is their mother tongue. There is a huge influence from our parents that we all get from birth.

Your relationship with yourself is primarily based on what you discover during your childhood. In my case, I learned from what my grandparents knew and taught me. Since these were my first relationships, they had a huge influence on me, but as I started to discover myself, I started to look differently at my relationship with myself.

Now that I understand the influence that our parents/guardians can have in our lives, I know that you can overcome that influence when you get confidence in yourself and believe in who you are. It might take time to fully find your own authenticity, but in the end everything is possible.

I come from a society that follows their culture. A woman is not allowed to wear long trousers, as it is considered disrespectful. I have known this since I was a small child. I remember one time as a grown adult I visited my grandmother and made the mistake of wearing long trousers, and I got myself into big trouble. I was beaten for having disrespected my culture. To me, the way I was dressed did not mean rudeness or disrespect, I simply wanted to look pretty.

When I fell in love with my husband and made plans to marry him, I found lots of obstacles to marrying him. The love of my life was not Kenyan, not chosen by my parents, did not have the same religion, was older and was not black. I became the talk of the town, people looked down on me and I became an outcast. This whole situation made me feel ashamed. I felt like I had broken taboos. I was even told that I had embarrassed my family for choosing to marry a man from a different culture.

In my culture it is difficult to make your own decisions about whom you can love and whom you can marry. But, as I became more and more confident that it is me who is in charge of my destiny and myself, I followed my heart and married him. Unfortunately, this step created a new distance between my father and me. I had disappointed him by not following my culture. The fact that I was born out of wedlock meant I was supposed to marry a man from the same clan, so that I could sanctify myself. I am not sure if this is a religious or cultural belief, but whichever it is, I have never understood why the sin of my having been born out of wedlock was put back onto me.

There have been moments in my life where I asked myself: where is God? I was very bitter with my life and how I have been viewed as a human being. I did not understand that people who are very strict in their own beliefs would be so judgemental as to try to destroy someone else's existence. I believe that God wants to see me happy, and that is the very reason for my existence. He knew me even before I was created. Based on all my confusion about my culture and my religious beliefs, there were moments when I would question my faith. Although I was born and raised as a Muslim, I do not consider myself to be religious, but I am spiritual. I have always considered that there is only one God, who is equal for all religions. As being a Muslim did not really inspire me, I felt free to explore other religions, and I eventually found that the Christian church inspired me more than my own religion. And again, because I was confident that I am in charge and can make my own decisions, I decided to get baptised.

CHAPTER 8: Searching for One's Happiness

Even today, I do not regret this step, but I do appreciate that people can have different religions but still have a relationship together.

To me, God is love. It is not what we have done or not done that makes us more sinful or righteous in His eyes. He wants us to be happy. A few years back I took a step toward reconciling with my father, since in African culture a parent will never say they are sorry. To do so is to give your own child power, which is considered not okay. During our conversations, his response was that it was my mum who was responsible for everything that happened, and so she should be the one to solve it. My heart was bleeding in pain as my mum had so little to do with my life, and I felt he was passing the blame.

I personally believe that we are all responsible for our own actions and someday when I die, I will be the one in charge of how I lived my life. I am sure God will be happy to know that I have lived the life that he had planned for me before I was even conceived. But before then, I love and approve of myself for being me, for following my own path and living a life that gives me happiness and not one that impresses other people. I may have been an embarrassment to my family but one thing that I know is that all things work together for good for those who believe in God.

Here is a love letter to my future self:

> Dear Fauza,
>
> It is my absolute pleasure to write these words to you. I hope that you are full of power and are now fearless. I know you struggled to find yourself, you were full of anger and disappointment and did not love yourself fully. You lived your life not accepting who you really were based on what was happening in your life.

I am sending you these words today just to remind you of how beautiful you are and how strong and powerful you are. I would love for you to know that life is so beautiful. You have a handsome and loving son who is healthy and loves you unconditionally, a loving husband who loves you for who you are; you are healthy and your family is healthy too.

I would love for you to know that what happens in our life is for us to learn; these life journeys are there to shape us. When something happens that we did not expect, the first thing we should ask ourselves is: what am I going to learn from this situation? Looking on the negative side of it will never change the problem; instead we should be grateful that this problem has happened, because only once we do so will we come out from the other side very bold and full of wisdom.

You are such a loving and caring person, your friends are inspired by you and you have so many goals that you want to achieve. I want to tell you that everything is possible if you believe and trust that God will guide you along the way.

The future is very bright. Let go of all your worries and fears, love those who love you and let go of those who don't. Live your life fully and love the woman you have become because you have so much power within you, so let your torch shine.

With love and kindness,

The fearless Fauza

CHAPTER NINE

Trust Your Gut Instinct

'I've come to trust not that events will always unfold exactly as I want, but that I will be fine either way. The challenges we face in life are always lessons that serve our soul's growth.'

Marianne Williamson

CHAPTER NINE
Trust Your Gut Instinct

When I was a little girl I had many dreams, but many times I doubted myself based on my own fear. There were moments when I believed that I was born with my own uniqueness and potential but, based on my own limiting thoughts, some of the dreams lost their power. I never had someone to guide me or empower me to be confident with myself. When I look at my younger self I see a girl who was full of fear, she didn't believe in herself. She had low self-esteem and no confidence at all. I thought it was impossible to trust anybody, and I was in fear of the people around me.

What is confidence and what is trust? In my way of thinking I look at confidence as accepting that what you did and do is good. It is a way of living. I look at trust as believing that the people around you have the best intent for you. When we do not have confidence in ourselves, we lose our own authenticity. When we are afraid, we forget who we are and forget the purpose of our existence. We often look at what is happening around us and define ourselves through that.

I believe that we are all born with our own uniqueness and potential, but sometimes only a few people manage to realise who they really are. So often we get caught up doing things that we don't love. But to realise our purpose we must be ready to really listen to ourselves or even sometimes to seek guidance from professionals. When I look to myself I would say the starting point of my professional life was chosen based on fear. It did not come from love. I realised this when I was struggling with what I was doing. But I have learned to have confidence in myself and by achieving this, I have slowly gained more and more trust that whatever I do will achieve a better me.

'Don't allow what others say have the power to ruin you, it's more about them, less about you. A reflection of what they are going through.'

Unknown

Understanding ourselves

Why do we hang on to our limited thinking when it creates unhappiness in our lives? I don't see any logical reason as to why we should continue to think in ways that bring us misery.

I believe that we are all created with a supernatural power, but so often we lose that as we get older. When a baby is born their mind is blank. It is the duty of the parents or guardians to fill the innocent child's vase with positive thoughts. But when we are surrounded by negative minds, that's what we will grow up hearing and knowing and that has an impact on our future.

We are always dealing with our thoughts but what I did not know was that I could change how I feel when I changed how I think. I lived my entire childhood thinking that I would not make it in life and that I was a failure, just because someone else said so. I didn't know I had the power to change how I felt. We are all responsible for our own feelings and thoughts and it is only by practising thinking differently that we can be happy.

Battling with the different emotions of lacking an identity was not easy for me. I was running away from my emotions. I think I did what children do, blame themselves for having that kind of life. I lived my life as best as I could but I was not fully alive. It took me years to learn to appreciate and to love myself, and by doing this, I began to think differently. I created a new style of thinking so that, when the negative thoughts started, I would tell myself how beautiful I am and how God took His time to mould me because there is only one person that looks like me and that's me.

CHAPTER 9: Trust Your Gut Instinct

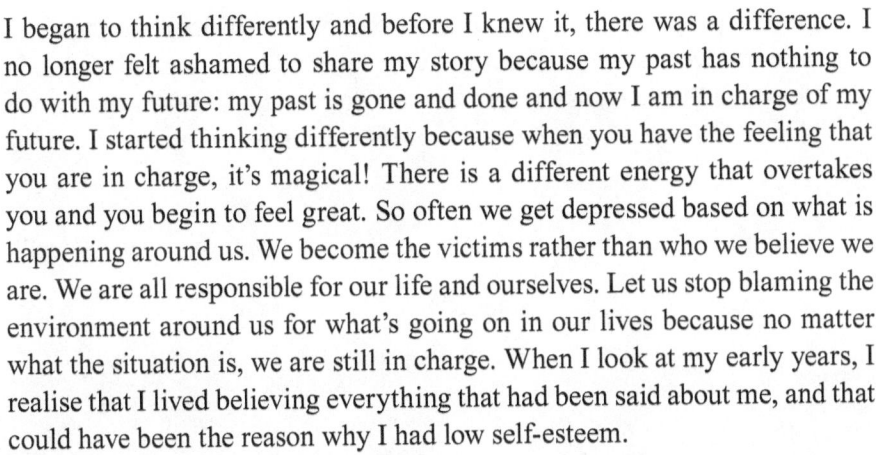

I began to think differently and before I knew it, there was a difference. I no longer felt ashamed to share my story because my past has nothing to do with my future: my past is gone and done and now I am in charge of my future. I started thinking differently because when you have the feeling that you are in charge, it's magical! There is a different energy that overtakes you and you begin to feel great. So often we get depressed based on what is happening around us. We become the victims rather than who we believe we are. We are all responsible for our life and ourselves. Let us stop blaming the environment around us for what's going on in our lives because no matter what the situation is, we are still in charge. When I look at my early years, I realise that I lived believing everything that had been said about me, and that could have been the reason why I had low self-esteem.

'We all have moments of loneliness and isolation. It takes courage to open up, be vulnerable, and allow others into our lives. But by doing so we can in fact allow others to help us through our challenges.'

Brene Brown

I used to be so afraid to tell people who I really was. I was afraid of being judged. I used to think if people knew who I really was they would think I was that girl who everyone thinks is a prostitute.

People can judge even before they know you. It was a struggle: there were moments I would not tell the truth for fear of getting more labels. I am very grateful to my friend Bernice who taught me that fear is merely the thoughts we create in our minds. And no matter what has happened, never be a victim. Life is a journey and when we face obstacles the only way to heal ourselves is by accepting and embracing reality. We need to learn to let go of our uncertainty and love who we are instead of giving our power away, because that is what the enemy wants: to break us. It is not our responsibility to change how people see us. And as much as it can be difficult we shouldn't expect to be loved by people the way we love them. I have come to a place in my life where I have realised that the most important relationship is the one that I have with myself, and every other relationship is optional.

'Take pride in how far you have come and have faith in how far you can go.'

Unknown

All things work together for the better. I remember when I was asked to leave home to get a place for myself with just the little money that I had, I was scared and did not know how things would turn out. The fear of the unknown is what breaks some of us. But what if we could change our thoughts and think that from all this confusion something good is going to happen? Sometimes when things seem not to be moving in the direction we want, we tend to curse the situation. It's quite normal because we are fighting or reacting against the situation. Difficulties in life present opportunities for us to learn. At every single moment we are given the opportunity to choose, and whatever decision we make today will determine what we will face next. We mustn't be afraid to create peace with ourselves. Whatever the situation in which we find ourselves, we can find answers if we stay calm and not panic. When we have peace with ourselves we can be sure that the decisions we make will work out in our favour.

CHAPTER TEN

Becoming Empowered

> *'You can't get to courage without walking through vulnerability.'*
>
>
>
> Brene Brown

CHAPTER 10: Becoming Empowered

CHAPTER TEN
Becoming Empowered

Anyone can give up. It's the easiest thing to do. But to hold yourself together when everyone expects you to fall apart: that is true strength. If I knew when I was a little girl that letting go and loving myself would help me in letting go of my uncertainty, I would have done so many years back. As a young girl I did not know what lay ahead but, as the saying goes, every cloud has a silver lining. All of our experiences, no matter how awful they seem to be, are temporary. It is how we react that makes a difference.

I have learned to look at any experience and ask myself how I can use this for my own growth. Acceptance of an experience as a temporary situation can make it a lot easier to handle. Loving ourselves has nothing to do with being selfish. Loving ourselves is about accepting who we are and taking responsibility for our own development, growth and happiness.

Do you believe that you deserve to be happy? If you don't, you can't allow yourself to be happy. Circumstances beyond your control will arise just to frustrate you. Loving yourself isn't something that happens overnight and it may not come easy to all of us. It didn't for me when I started loving myself; it was very difficult at first, but in any situation I believe we have the choice to love or fear. Fear is the reason we find it hard to love ourselves completely. But what we should know is that everything in life that has happened to you - even the disappointments - are for you to learn from and they may perhaps guide you to a different destination. Even the closed doors help make you into who you are today.

In life it is important to keep our hearts free from hate. We are told to love our enemies but the act of forgiving does not necessary mean we must accept all sorts of things. We should especially not accept things that do not comply with our values, because if we do that we lose focus of our dreams.

'Sense of worthiness - that critically important piece that gives us access to love and belonging - lives inside of our story.'

Brene Brown

My turning point came about when I stopped running away from what was happening and faced my demons. Sometimes what we need is to have closure with the things that are tormenting us. This is the only way to leave the past behind and move on with life.

It was on a Christmas Eve and as usual we were exchanging gifts in my family. It is one of our rituals; we exchange letters and gifts with each other. One of the gifts my husband gave me was a book. This was a surprise, as I had expected something totally different but I have to say this was the best gift as it helped me to stop thinking of myself as a victim with everything that had happened. I remember opening my gift and it was a copy of Louise Hay's book, *You Can Heal Your Life*.

It was after reading this book I realised that everything that happened to me were just lessons to make me a better person. All of our life experiences are different - I cannot say mine were more difficult than someone else's - but it is up to us to choose how we look at the experiences we go through in life. We can look at each of them as experiences, or we can make ourselves get stuck in the past. We have the choice to make.

When I look at my past life, the reason why I was not moving forward was because I used to look at my past and feel sorry for what had happened. What I did not know was that I am responsible for my own happiness. I had to forgive myself for punishing myself and for all the perceived wrongs in order

CHAPTER 10: Becoming Empowered

to set myself free. I forgave my past, and in return I have been given this beautiful life that I have been living for the last couple of years. I feel very light. I always compare it to setting a caged bird free and seeing how they fly with so much freedom. I started looking at life with a different view after I chose to love myself and be happy with who I am and how far I have come. When I look back, I see a different woman who is full of self-love.

I believe in the power of love. It is magical when you have a sense of love and belonging. Everything around you feels and looks different, you start attracting like-minded people and people start smiling at you when you pass them. Do you know why? It is because you are attracting good things as you are a loving person and because you are in a positive mood. I remember that I started having a lot of ideas on how I could develop myself. I started tapping into my goals and the whole world changed. I really do not see any value any more in depression or feeling powerless.

We can only gain power and confidence by being willing to change. If we spend our whole lives wondering why certain things happened to us, we will always be living in the past. You can't help yourself or others if you look inward and feel sorry for yourself. I believe that we have to change ourselves every day to go out and make the world a better place.

When I look at myself there are moments when I wish that I lived my life fully, and there are moments when I sometimes feel like I have wasted the first part of my life. I have lived nearly the whole of my last 20 years in darkness. I believed everything that I was told about myself (although sometimes I was unaware of it) and I feared failure, rejection, the unknown, isolation and not being in control. I convinced myself that everything that was happening in my life was caused by something or someone outside my life. What I didn't know was that when we master our fears, we become courageous and fear does not exist: fear is only thoughts we create ourselves.

'Some people succeed because they are destined, but most succeed because they are determined.'

Henry Van Dyke

CHAPTER ELEVEN

Choosing a Career

CHAPTER ELEVEN
Choosing a Career

What is the spark in your heart that makes you happy? We need to know what really excites us by having a deep conversation with ourselves before settling for anything. When I look at myself, I have moved from one job to another because I have never felt like I loved what I was doing. Initially I was just working to have the financial freedom to pay my bills but I used to go to my work without any energy.

It is quite normal in some Kenyan families that the first-born child tries to meet the expectations of their parents by entering the career your parents think is good for you. Fortunately for me, I did not have the grades after finishing high school that were required for joining the army. If you ask me now, I am so grateful that I couldn't join the army. I decided to do hotel management because I thought this would be work I'd like, meeting and serving guests in the hotel industry.

Was it easy to change career? No! So often we live a life of misfortune because we find ourselves doing work that deep down in our heart we know we really don't love. But taking a definite step to change is very difficult as you step from the known into the unknown. It wasn't until I moved to Dubai that I found out what the baby inside me really loved. When we got our house in Dubai I decorated it myself and found out that I loved to be creative. Based on this discovery I went back to school to study interior design.

It's never too late to find yourself and to set another goal. We all know what we want and sometimes it might take time before we fully realise our calling, but what I have learnt through my own experience is that we all have the capability to strive for what we truly want. As Oprah Winfrey says,

CHAPTER 11: Choosing a Career

'with every experience, you alone are painting your own canvas, thought by thought, choice by choice.'

I learnt in my 20s that lots of people live their lives saying 'I wish I knew what I wanted to do' or 'I wish I could do this or that' without taking the action to do it! We must be the captain of our own ships. There is one rule that I always try to embrace and that is if I have something I want to do, regardless of what it is, I will do it even if the whole world says no. I have learned to say yes to myself and to follow my own path. If you believe in yourself and have trust in God, no matter how long it may take, one day it will come to pass.

'To be yourself in a world
that is constantly trying
to make you something
else is the greatest thing
you will ever do.'

Brene Brown

CHAPTER TWELVE

Finding True Love

CHAPTER TWELVE
Finding True Love

I lived all my early life in fear. I was very self-conscious in everything that I did because I did not want to be hurt. I did not trust anyone based on my life experiences. Because of my own struggles of self-love I needed to protect my feelings so that no one would hurt me.

I first met my husband in 2008. At first there was no relationship; we were friends for a couple of years before we both found out that there was more than just friendship. I was conscious that it was taboo in my culture to make decisions by myself, so I went to my father to tell him about my love friendship. Parents must be informed, as children are not supposed to make decisions for themselves, even when they are adults. And because I was very conscious of taking any authority, I informed one of my uncles and one of my father's friends.

My uncle, together with my father's friend and I, went to my father to share the good news. I walked into my father's home, and Dad was welcoming and happy to see me. I remember sitting down in his living room and I started telling him that I had found my life partner. He was concerned with the idea of his daughter marring a foreigner, which is normal for a parent, but after hours of questions from my father he understood and blessed me and wished me the very best in my relationship. I was happy to receive my father's blessing, but received a text message from him weeks later stating that he would not allow me to get married. When I received that news I was shocked to my last nerve, and I knew this was not his decision but came from his family and relatives.

CHAPTER 12: Finding True Love

'Choosing authenticity is not an easy choice. To be nobody but yourself in a world which is doing its best day and night to make you like everybody else, means to fight the hardest battle which any human being can fight and never stop fighting, but staying real is one of the most courageous battles that we will ever fight.'

Brene Brown

Talking to my father made me realise that I had done my part. I knew I had done what kids should do and I was truly grateful to my father for his blessings. I know he wanted me to get married to a man of the same ethnicity as myself but unfortunately that was not to be the case.

My husband is my rock. He loves me for who I am. He has literally seen me grow from a teenage girl who was full of fear to becoming a confident woman. It is a blessing to have a partner who is very supportive and who encourages me to find my own authentic self. My husband has had a huge impact on my life, helping me to know the meaning of love and how to love others, helping me to accept myself and to live my life fully with no regrets or fears. He also mirrors me sometimes, but I know he does it with good intentions. I am truly grateful for the gift of my husband and thank God for giving me a man who is so lovable.

We got married and a new life started and a year later God blessed us with our son. Jasper changed everything in our life. Although being a first time mum can sometimes be a challenge, and at the same time joyous, I needed to be the best mother I could be for our son. I had made a vow with myself that the day God blessed me with a child I would try to be the best mother that I could, and I would give all the love to my child that I never had myself while growing up.

Having a partner who is from a different culture and looks at things differently has helped me to appreciate diversity in cultures and to have a more open mind. I realise that I have to look at certain things from different points of view; after all, we are all connected by the same universe. We are one and there is only one race and that's the human race.

A new world opened up for me. I have travelled the world and the opportunity to travel and see different countries with their different cultures has opened my eyes. I started looking at my own past as a learning experience, and I started looking at things differently. It is by accepting and appreciating others that we also get to learn from them.

CHAPTER THIRTEEN

My Expat Life in Dubai

'I am not the same,
having seen the moon
shine on the other side of
the world.'

Mary Anne Radmacher

CHAPTER THIRTEEN
My Expat Life in Dubai

If you had told me years ago that someday I would travel and see the world I would not have believed you. When you have no faith in life, hope disappears. What a dream to be able to live in one of the best cities in the world.

The UAE is an inspirational country to live in. I love Dubai. I am so grateful to have had the chance to step foot in this country. I always say how lucky I am to live in a country so many people dream of visiting. Dubai is a beautiful city with so many things to learn from.

I had never thought of living in Dubai because just the thought of coming here was so like a dream that I was not sure it would ever be a reality. We moved to Dubai six years ago when my husband started his new job. When my husband got his job we were given a DVD to watch with tips on starting a new life in Dubai. It was such an exciting moment. What made me marvel was the fact that there are people from more than 150 different nationalities living here. I was amazed to learn what a multicultural city it is.

Although the excitement was there, there were moments when I was in doubt as to how I would settle and feel at home in a big city. I did not know anyone apart from my family. We started our adventure in 2011, and two days after our arrival my husband had to start his new job and I had to take care of our son who was only 14 months old. Being a stay-at-home-mum in a big city with no social network was not easy at all, and there were moments when I felt like maybe we should not have made this decision. I was depressed and had no friends, and it was a challenge. I felt like a part of my life had been taken away, my social life.

RISING FROM THE DUST

My life started when I met my new neighbour. I remember I was playing outside our house with my 14 month old son one afternoon when a lady walked by and greeted me. She stopped and introduced herself to me and said, 'Oh! You have a handsome young man!' about my son, Jasper. She mentioned that she was my neighbour. At first, I wondered how she could see the resemblance between my son and I as there have been times when I was asked if I was my son's nanny.

I felt like an angel had been sent to me. Wendy was very kind to tell me that if there was any help that I needed to settle in my new city she was more than happy to help me. A new relationship began. I could go to her house at any time and she would open the door for me and help me with any information that I needed. I am so grateful to have met such a lovely neighbour because, as the saying goes, 'a good neighbour is better than a far friend'.

As time went by I started feeling at home in my new city, and a year later when Jasper was in kindergarten, I had a lot of free time. I started getting bored with the everyday routine of being a stay-at-home-mum. Although there was so much to do in the house I had no idea how I could make our house into a home, and I wanted to learn how. Being an expat is a beautiful thing as there are opportunities to develop yourself, and since I had a couple of hours every day to myself, I decided to learn something rather than just doing nothing every day.

In the midst of searching the internet for short courses I could do, I came across an expat website and that's where all the magic was. I got all the answers to my questions. Months later I started taking interior design workshops and through attending these classes I met other women. Some of them were new to the city just like myself and were also filling in the free hours that they had to develop themselves. Some had been living in the city for many years and wanted to tap into their passion for creativity. I continued taking the workshops and a new passion developed, and a year later I decided to go back to college to complete a higher diploma in interior design.

CHAPTER 13: My Expat Life in Dubai

Ever since then there has never been a dull moment. This reminds me of a quote from HH Sheik Mohammed bin Rashid Al Maktoum, who says, 'In Dubai we don't wait for things to happen, we make them happen'. It is very true: the city is full of positive energy and you get inspired from everywhere. The positive energy inspires you so much that you don't want to sit and do nothing.

Juggling being a mum and wanting to develop myself was a challenge, but I have learnt to prioritize and do only the things that are important. We have to make some serious decisions not to jeopardise anything while at the same time having a balanced life style. As the saying goes, 'everything is possible if you put your mind to it'.

'Every experience is a success.'

Louise Hay

We do not need to beat ourselves up when something goes wrong. Instead, we need to look at each failure as a learning experience.

What does failure mean anyway? Does it mean that something did not turn out in our favour? If so, that is not the end of life. We must understand that through all this confusion something good will come. We must train our minds to look at each situation with a positive attitude, for it is only by doing so that we create peace with ourselves.

When searching for one's personal path, there are many obstacles along the way and if you don't believe in yourself and have faith that in the end things will turn out to be great, you can easily get discouraged. A few years ago when I had just started my jewellery collection, I nearly gave up. When I came up with the idea to create jewellery, I didn't know how I would sell it, but I knew anything was possible. I started approaching some online shops to see if I could use their platforms for selling, but unfortunately, I was told that my designs did not match with their products. This was fair enough, but it started me thinking what bad luck. I did not give up, however, and approached more sites, but the answer was the same: 'sorry, your designs do not suit our products'. I started questioning whether what I was doing suited the market, but I did not want just to call it off. As the saying goes, 'if at first you don't succeed, try and try again'. I remember telling myself that a great deal was coming for me but I did not know what it was and how long it would take.

Sometimes what seems to be a big tragedy turns out to become the greatest thing in our lives. You don't have to be great to start, but you have to start to be great.

Everything in life is a process. Events occur one at a time until the process is complete and we are ready to move to the next level. When we are facing any difficulty in life, the question we must first ask ourselves is which is the way forward? What are the steps I can take to begin working through and out of this situation? It's only by doing so we are able to get clarity on really what we want. Although I did not know how I would go about it all, I believed that everything is possible. No matter how long it took, someday things would fall into place. As the saying goes, 'Rome wasn't built in a day.'

It took me quite some time before I could figure out the best way to market my collection. And that's when BIF (Beltz Inspiration by Fauza) was born from my frustration and rejection. I decided I was the only person who could make the change that I sought.

I love to inspire other people, especially women. I believe that when women inspire and support each other we can do so much together as a team. The reason I started BIF was because I needed a place where other women could login and get valuable information. When my jewellery was rejected from the other websites, I knew I was the only one who could make the impossible

CHAPTER 13: My Expat Life in Dubai

possible, and I believed that I couldn't just let people dim the light of my dream. BIF started as a blog where I blogged about interior design, fashion, my own jewellery and sometimes about self-love. After all the refusals I received, I knew what I wanted and I believed if I worked a bit harder, my persistence and determination and positive attitude would get me what I needed. I had learned that sometimes rejection is just a signal that the road we are about to take isn't good for us. But we must be ready in mind, body and spirit before we can make a change.

It has taken me many months to get a place to stock my jewellery but, as the saying goes, 'good things come to those who wait'. After trial and error, I managed to find a boutique to stock my jewellery. I have learned to be patient and that when you believe in yourself and your product, no matter how long it takes, in the end everything will fall into place. Other people cannot convince us to do it: we are in charge of what matters in our life. And if we believe that something is possible, the universe will conspire and make it happen in our favour. It may take time but there is always a light at the end of the tunnel.

'There is no passion to be found playing small, in settling for a life that is less than the one you are capable of.'

Nelson Mandela

We are responsible for the changes we want to see in our lives. It is easier to just sit back and wait for a miracle to happen but this might never occur and we will only be blaming ourselves or even the universe for what is happening in our lives. When I was searching for my own spark and nothing was making sense, I remember watching Oprah in one of her videos. She was emphasising that 'we are the only ones responsible for our lives and if we sit around waiting for people to fix us or help us, we are wasting our time'. This made me realise that I was not living the life that inspires me. If I wanted to see a difference in my life then I had to change my game.

What made me start living my life with intention is when I came to the realization that there was more to life than settling for less. I realised that my purpose in life was greater than the life I was living. It is okay that sometimes we may not know how to go about finding what we want, but in order for me to find my passion I needed to figure out who I wanted to be and what inspired me. I knew what triggered my enthusiasm, but I did not know how to go about it. Being an expert is a great thing, but with all the advantages there are some disadvantages, too. Sometimes you may have a great idea but it might be hard to achieve it for many different reasons. It can be frustrating.

I remember reading *The Alchemist* and the author says we all need to be aware of our personal calling. I started thinking and asking myself: am I living the life that God has chosen for me? Is it fulfilling? Am I happy with who I am? What is it that is holding me back? Although I had so many questions with no answers, I needed to come up with a game plan. It took me a great deal of time before I could figure out what it was that I needed and how I could go about it, and that is why I decided to get a personal coach.

Sometimes we might have a million ideas, but if we don't have a vision and someone to guide us, we will always feel as if we are stuck. I remember walking into Amanda's office with a lot of frustrations, ideas, questions and fears. Although I did not have a vision, I knew the woman I wanted to become. I am a person who likes juggling different things and that's why I get frustrated easily, especially if things are not working out well. But in all that I do I always make sure that I am always there for my family.

I am a qualified interior designer and I also have my own jewellery collection. My jewellery is inspired by the Masai of Kenya. All the pieces are very traditional and I design them to suit every woman. I have always been a fan of playing dress-up and I always feel good when I see a woman looking

CHAPTER 13: My Expat Life in Dubai

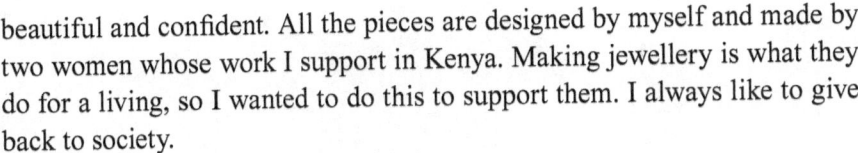

beautiful and confident. All the pieces are designed by myself and made by two women whose work I support in Kenya. Making jewellery is what they do for a living, so I wanted to do this to support them. I always like to give back to society.

'A lot of people have gone further than they thought they could because someone else thought they could.'

Unknown

CHAPTER FOURTEEN

The Importance of Mentors

CHAPTER FOURTEEN
The Importance of Mentors

I strongly believe we need mentors or life coaches. When I look at myself, I know that if I had never had the right mentors or the friends to encourage me and want to see me succeed, then perhaps my ideas would still be in the back of my mind. In order for someone to succeed they need to be guided, and that's why mentors are important. You may have a lot of ideas but sometimes you might not know how to go about bringing them to fruition, and it is mentors or coaches who can direct us.

Every successful person knows that they have to invest in mentoring or coaching at some point. These examples are pretty clear, even from the beginning of time. We have heard the great stories like that of Jesus, spending time learning the scriptures and listening to his teachers before He commenced His life as a teacher Himself. He also spent time learning from His father Joseph who was a carpenter. There are modern day examples like that of Serena Williams who is mentored by her sister, Venus Williams. There are other examples like Dr John Demartini, who has dedicated his life to teaching and travelling. He has been able to do so by finding his passion and developing something out of it. But he also mentions how he loves to read and research. He also puts emphasis on surrounding yourself with inspiring individuals.

Nelson Mandela is another great example. In his book, *The Long Walk to Freedom,* he mentions that he was not born an activist and that he felt inadequate among people who knew and understood politics. Even Mandela had to learn from the best and be mentored in the areas he needed mentoring.

Sometimes mentors come in the form of friends or siblings, but sometimes you have to reach out and find people to come on board to mentor you.

CHAPTER 14: The Importance of Mentors

I remember during one of my conversations with Nkandu, she insisted on finding someone who has walked your path to help you accomplish your vision. In a recent conversation I had with Nkandu on mentoring she told me her story. When she was in high school, she loved to write. She wanted to become a journalist but didn't know how to start. So upon completion of high school, armed with a letter of recommendation, Nkandu went to ask for a job at Ngami Times Newspaper in Maun Botswana. She told me how nervous she was but she still went ahead, stepping into the editor's office who also happened to be the owner of the business. Sometimes what we fear the most can turn out to be the greatest achievement in our lives. Nkandu was given a chance to start working and for her to rise higher she needed mentoring and coaching. She asked for a mentor. She was given someone within the organisation but they didn't click well. I believe their personalities didn't match. So Nkandu went back to the editor who was right at the top of the organisation, and he recommended she contact the director of the Media Institute of Southern Africa. She tells me that it was one of the best things that ever happened to her. Not only did the director help her with connections, he also taught her how to navigate the journalism industry. It is very important to know what you want and ask for it.

One of the best things about having mentors is that they have a different skill set. Having someone you can bounce off ideas is great, but that is what friends are for. You need to find a skilled mentor, someone who has a different set of skills to you, and someone you can learn from. Sometimes these people act as coaches and you might have to pay a coaching fee. The question to ask always is: will I see a return on my investment? What is this person teaching me? Does his or her life demonstrate what I am being taught? Sometimes you can embody great leaders. The purpose is to learn something. You can also obtain certain skills through reading books. For example, if you want to run a business in hair or cosmetics, you should start by reading business books and talking to people who are in the industry. Once you decide that this is what you want to do, you start doing the training and once you finish you get someone who is successful in their industry to teach you the ins and outs of the business. This concept applies to everything we do, whether it be sports, writing books or running your own medical clinic. You need to have a mentor or a coach who is demonstrating what they are teaching. Someone once said 'getting advice from certain people is like asking Steve Wonder for directions'. Be careful who you listen to and what practical advice they give you. Make sure you evaluate it and always trust your gut.

CHAPTER FIFTEEN

Be Open to New Opportunities

USEFUL OPPORTUNITIES

'The secret to unlocking your potential is recognizing an opportunity and having the courage to use it.'

Heddie Goldberg

CHAPTER FIFTEEN
Be Open to New Opportunities

We must always be on the lookout for new opportunities. When I was done with college, I needed to do something. I remember asking myself: now that I am done with college, how am I going to use this knowledge? I have always wished to start my own business but I did not know how to go about it. In 2015, just when I was done with college, I was not able to get a part-time job, as working full time was not an option for me, but it didn't work out well.

I felt frustrated. I was stressed and I started going back to my old way of thinking that I was a failure. In the midst of all this, as I was searching the internet about how I could start my own interior design consultancy, I landed on my friend's Facebook page where she had posted information about an organization that was offering business funding. I looked at it and I remember jumping onto their website. I read what it was all about and told myself to give it a try. I told myself that it's less about winning than the knowledge and exposure that comes from it, and I saw it as an opportunity for me to learn.

I immediately registered and waited for their reply, and a day later I received confirmation that I was eligible for the Ro'Ya initiative, a Dubai Business Women's Council and MasterCard initiative to empower and encourage upcoming female entrepreneurs in the United Arab Emirates.

A new adventure began. I remember walking in the room, and the room was full of women whom were also eager to learn business skills. Some of them were already in the business world and some - like myself - were looking at starting.

On that first day I was uncertain. I did not know what to expect, but I walked in the room with an open mind, ready to learn. Working with the mentors, guest speakers and other women throughout the workshops was enlightening. Maria and Klaus from growme.ae shared a lot of knowledge with the Ro'ya women. They have moulded me as an individual into a more dynamic businesswoman.

Ro'Ya empowered me to strengthen my vision and the direction of my business so that I could move forward, building my brand with confidence and clarity. Sometimes when opportunities present themselves to you, all you need to do is to grab them and be grateful for the opportunity. As the saying goes, 'knowledge is power and no one will ever take it from you'. As it was my first time attending such an empowerment program, not only did I learn how to start a business from the beginning but also my experience in a social setting helped me a lot.

CHAPTER SIXTEEN

Inspiring Women

'When a woman succeeds she reaches out to those around her and pulls them up with her. That's why if you empower a woman, you are empowering a whole society.'

Queen Rania

CHAPTER SIXTEEN
Inspiring Women

Women have so many different facets: we all have our own personalities; we are strong; we are mums; we are wives; we are daughters; we are girlfriends; we are best friends; we are granddaughters. I love being a woman. My heart feels such gratitude to the women who have taken the courage to pave ways for other women. It really does take a lot of love to be able to inspire others. To see them find their own ways to succeed with their life, their goals and their careers. I am grateful for all the women in my circle who have all have an impact in my life.

Since I have known truly who I am, I have always wanted to share my story but I never knew how to go about it. I don't think I was ready to do so until 2015. It is true that what we desire the universe conspires to make possible because we are thinking positive thoughts. But sometimes things can happen only when we are ready for them.

In February 2015 I met Nkandu in person for the first time. We had been communicating for many years but it was something special to meet her in person for the first time.

Nkandu is one woman who I know loves seeing other people unleash their potential. One afternoon in 2015 while she was visiting me we had a small tour to downtown Dubai. It was almost lunch time and we sat down at one of my favourite restaurants for a meal together. As we were talking, she mentioned that she would love for me to be in her next project. Well, I must say I thought it was a joke. The news came to me so unexpectedly at the very moment I was going through my own crisis, with trying to find a part-time job and my jewellery not being accepted to different online platforms.

RISING FROM THE DUST

A month later she called me and told me she wanted me to be one of the women in her book *Fierce and Fabulous: the Feminine Force of Success*. As much as this was an opportunity for me, the baby in me was scared. I was not sure how people would resonate with hearing about a chapter of my life and that is what was scary, but I told myself to think positively and hope that out of ten people perhaps one person will benefit from what I shared.

Having part of my story featured in her book has enabled me travel to speak about myself, and has also empowered other people - especially women - to find their own authenticity. I remember a week after I attended the first *Fierce and Fabulous* book launch in Sydney in February 2016, I received messages from a few people who were there during the book launch. They told me they had read my story and they told me how my story resonated with them.

I was so grateful to know that people appreciated my story, and it is because of this that I felt the need to write my entire story. I will always be grateful to have had the opportunity to be in *Fierce and Fabulous: The Feminine Force of Success* as ever since my outlook towards myself has been better, knowing that I have inspired some people. I love the work that Nkandu is doing and the energy she puts into it. We all need people in our lives who can help us raise our standards, remind us of our essential purpose, and challenge us to become the best version of ourselves.

CHAPTER SEVENTEEN

Meeting Dr John Demartini

> *'Whatever we think about and thank about we bring about.'*
>
>
>
> Dr John Demartini

CHAPTER SEVENTEEN
Meeting Dr John Demartini

When I read *The Secret* and heard about the power of the universe and how thought creates things, I was amazed. I remember watching Dr John Demartini online and saying to myself that one day I would love to attend one of his speaking sessions.

One morning I was having one of my weekly Skype sessions with Nkandu to brainstorm my book and talk about my progress. On this particular morning we were having a chat about the book you are reading now, and about the book event in Melbourne for *Fierce and Fabulous: The Feminine Force of Success.*

A couple of weeks before my travels, I received an invitation from Nkandu to attend the Big-Think International Growth Forum for small businesses. Nkandu was one of the organizers of the event alongside John Di Natale, the founder of Big-Think. I knew Nkandu was hosting the event and John Di Natale and Finbar O'Hanlon would be speakers.

Nkandu is one of those types of people whose energy can be likened to that of a ball of fire. She makes things happen. The forum came about at a dinner table at the Sofitel when Di Natale talked about hosting Dr John Demartini. Nkandu said, 'I will make it happen'. So to my surprise she told me, 'this is happening, make sure your return flights give you enough room to spend a few extra days in Melbourne.'

It was only during our Skype conversation that I learnt Dr John Demartini would be speaking at the event too. At first I could not believe it, I remember asking Nkandu, 'am I dreaming? Is Dr John Demartini speaking for the Big-Think for Small Business event?'

Nkandu laughed and her answer was, 'yes!' I started thinking that our words have so much power and what we desire the universe conspires.

I remembered telling Nkandu early in 2016 when we were doing our weekly brainstorming sessions for this book that I would love to attend one of Dr John Demartini's speaking sessions 'someday'. I looked at her on my computer screen as we were Skype-ing, unaware that that 'someday' would be really very soon.

I am a big fan of Dr John Demartini and I have wanted to attend one of his sessions for a very long time. I vividly remember her telling me what we desire the universe conspires and because you are sending out positive thoughts that's what you will receive.

'The reality is that whatever you are looking for is, at the same time, looking for you. It all starts with believing before seeing.'

Dr John Demartini

On the morning of the event of the Big-Think International Growth Forum for small businesses, I remember walking in the room with enthusiasm, ready to learn from the speakers. The event started and Nkandu, who was MC, introduced all the speakers.

John Di Natale in his speech emphasised how we should think big, get focused and get things done. Finbar O'Hanlon emphasised the information detox that we need to learn to clear our minds so that we are able to shift our state and live for opportunities and inventions. Dr John Demartini shared his philosophy on how to tap into your genius and live a life that you truly deserve.

CHAPTER 17: Meeting Dr John Demartini

The forum was an amazing learning opportunity that I will always be grateful for. What I learned was that we are the only ones who limit ourselves. We often think we are inadequate, and we forget that we have the power to be all that we can be. We tend to limit ourselves even before we take the first step on our journey.

Here are some of the things that I took away with me during the session: I learned that when we are young we have many dreams, but as we grow, we lose our own light. This can be caused by the people around us. In order for us to grow as people we need to give ourselves permission to do extraordinary things on the planet. We all have a mission and it is impossible for us not to fulfil it, as it is our destiny. What I learned was that we need to document all the things that we are grateful for every day. This reminds me of a quote from Deepak Chopra, who says 'Gratitude opens the door to the power, the wisdom, the creativity of the universe. You open the door through gratitude'. When we give ourselves a low priority we are devaluing our genius and we shouldn't let anything distract us from our vision. It is the challenges in life that make us stronger. Challenges create genius.

Epilogue

We have only one life to live. Think of this for a moment.

No matter what has happened in your life, what makes it different is what you do with your past to create the life you are living at the moment. Writing this book has given me a better understanding of my personal life. Understanding life comes only with experience as nobody gets instructions on how life is going to be. Therefore, we should not punish ourselves for whatever life throws at us. I have done that and I have learned my lessons.

Going through the process of writing this book has made me discover that sometimes we have to fully understand the truth of what has happened before we judge or conclude. However, a lot of times we do not get all the answers to our questions and we have to learn to accept that. I have learned through my life experiences that there is no point punishing yourself for things that you cannot change.

At the very beginning of my life, I had so much anger to my parents for not being the perfect parents as I probably had seen in a Hollywood television program. I had blamed my parents for their own life choices. But now I understand that we all make mistakes and we do not need to punish others or even ourselves for the choices we make in life. No one is perfect. We are all in this thing called life, and sometimes we fall, but how we rise is what will make the difference, it can either shape us or destroy us.

Imagine if we could love ourselves a little more. Love ourselves with no fear, judgement or guilt. When we are born we do not know anything about fear, anger, guilt or condemnation. We pick up all these limiting thoughts as we grow based on the experience we get from the people and society around us.

By writing this book, I have also realised that sometimes people do certain things based on the circumstances around them and that is perfectly fine. We have to learn to adjust ourselves along the way. When life gets hard, we need to remind ourselves that no one said life would always be rosy. Let us love ourselves a little more, which is the only way to live a happy life. Each of us has lived through some devastation or loneliness, and some have weathered physical or spiritual super storms. When we look at each other we must say, I understand how you feel because I have been there myself. We must support each other because each of us is more alike than we are unlike.

When you look at a person, any person, remember that everyone has a story. Everyone has gone through something that has changed them and that is the very reason why sometimes people behave in a certain way: because they are battling within themselves. Instead of judging them, let's find a way to know them because maybe they need our love and support.

I have learned to be grateful and content whatever the circumstances are. I know what it is to be in need and I know what it is to have plenty. I have also learned to put my trust in God as His way of doing things is really mysterious. I have walked without shoes and I have also taken a shower 40000 feet on the sky. Always remember God will never abandon His own children. When you are in trouble, never lose your self, instead seek God first and everything else will be added unto you.

Fauza Beltz

September 2016

BONUS CHAPTER

Fierce and Fabulous

'I can't change the direction of the wind, but I can adjust my sails to always reach my destination.'

Jimmy Dean

BONUS CHAPTER
Fierce and Fabulous

Here is what I had shared in my first interview with Nkandu. You will find the exact transcript with that of 15 other women in the *Fierce and Fabulous: The Feminine Force of Success* – a book by Nkandu Beltz.

Fauza Beltz is a freelance interior designer and the owner and founder of BIF accessories. She believes it's not who you wear but what you wear. Her greatest passion is finding ways to live a life with intention and inspiring others to do the same.

Fauza is my sister in-law. We both married into the Beltz family. I had heard of her way before I met her. Even though this book mainly focuses on women in Australia, I needed to share her story. To me, Fauza embodies courage and resilience, love and success. Despite having a rough life, she has grown into a loving woman running an international business. She is one young lady to look out for. Nkandu Beltz

Nkandu: Tell me about your early life.

Fauza: I was born out of wedlock. My parents hadn't planned for me. As a result, my dad had no desire to live with my mother, and my mum wanted to get on with her life. I grew up in different homes. First, I was raised by my maternal grandmother in the village of Kwale (Mombasa) in Kenya. I'll always be grateful to her, but it was a tough childhood.

RISING FROM THE DUST

When I was five, my paternal grandmother took me in, and I started a new life with her as my mum. But even here, I received no love. She always beat me. Even though I had expected love from her as the only person I lived with, that was not in the picture, so I had to fight for myself.

By the age of seven I could cook and wash my own clothes. I became mature, because I had to. I felt out of place when I saw families together, but then I just had to make up my mind to get used to it. What I missed most in my childhood was the love. There was no moment in my childhood when I would say I had a family that loved me.

I was in a day school that was two hours away on foot. I used to leave the house at six am and return by about five thirty. When I got back home, most of the time there was no lunch. I'd go get the *ugali* (maize flour cooked with water to porridge) or maybe there was *cassava* or yams. Whatever was there, I'd help myself to it. I decided early on not to whine about it all of the time, because it did me no good.

When I finished primary school, my father took me to a boarding school close to Nairobi. It was there a new chapter began for me. I met people detached from their parents and started to create some friendships. I only went home during holidays, although the word *home* might not be accurate, in the way most people consider it. I had to stay with my stepmother, who also didn't treat me as family. She always reminded me I was just a stepdaughter and therefore inferior to her own daughters. The only persons who welcomed me were the neighbours. One of them, Bernice, is still one of my best friends.

After boarding school, I studied at college and stayed with a cousin in Nairobi, as I no longer felt welcome in my stepmother's house. Because of this, I again had to walk two hours back and forth to school. After college, I started my working life as a waitress. I didn't have any money to buy a uniform, but Bernice helped me. In my second job as a hotel hostess, I met my husband who showed an interest in me and didn't seem to care where I came from. A year into our relationship, I got pregnant. We married, and I decided that when I became a mother, everything would be different for my child, who would grow up with love.

Nkandu: How did becoming a wife and mother change you?

Fauza: My husband and son gave me a new life. They gave me confidence to accept me for who I am. A woman people listen to. Motherhood has given me this zeal. I will always be there for my son in good and bad times. I have an open mind and tell myself it sometimes doesn't matter what's right, and my past has nothing to do with the present. I am in charge. I am responsible for my life and the life of my child.

I guess this confidence came about after I realised how much power I had within me. It's up to me to decide what I want to do with my life. I spend a lot of time with my son, Jasper, and I try to teach him as much as I can about self-worth and how to be a loving person. I never want him to feel the way I did as a child. I love him dearly.

My husband is my best friend and my first mentor. He's a good listener and always gives his own opinion in an open, positive way that encourages me. I came to realise it doesn't matter what everyone thinks of you. In the end it's about who you believe you are. So if my family and I are all on the same page, it takes a blink of an eye to make a decision. It's that easy.

Nkandu: What message do you want to send by telling your story?

Fauza: I think it's important to tell my story if I can help someone who is where I used to be and thinks they can't do anything about it. When I look at my young self, I see a girl who was naive, insecure, and hopeless. The world looked black to her. But once I opened up and talked to people, I started to gain confidence. I realised I wasn't the only one.

RISING FROM THE DUST

Sometimes when we have a problem, we hold onto it and think it's the biggest problem in the world, and there's no way out.

What we all need to do is go out there and help someone who has an even bigger problem. It gets us out of feeling sorry for ourselves, and we can feel good in the process. I think it's important to be honest and let people know we need help. I've learnt if you don't ask, nobody will know what you really want or what you're going through. The reason I didn't tell anyone for a long time is because I was afraid of being judged. That was my biggest problem. It was only when I received love and had many talks with my husband that I realised my fear was created by myself and not by the environment. He taught me to convince myself it really doesn't matter.

For example, I participated in some workshops in Dubai. These conferences are focused on business development, and it's a great platform for networking and learning new skills for my business. When I got to the conference room, it felt like thirty well-dressed women were staring at me. I'm always a smart, casual mum who dresses for the occasion, but nowadays I don't mind how people look at me.

What I'm learning is to have an open mind. If someone or something comes into your life and it will help, grab it. Otherwise, just let it fly away. It takes a lot of courage to let go, but once you start loving and approving of yourself, everything falls into place. There's no greater love than the love you give to yourself.

I hope my story will help someone who has given up hope. I want to tell them that they are not who people say they are. They have so much power. I wouldn't want people to feel sorry for me. That's not my intention. I want them to know that sometimes situations are not what they seem. If we accept who we are, we can create peace within ourselves.

Fierce and Fabulous

Most of the time people feel bad because of self-doubt or lack of confidence. I mean, we all have that sometimes, but what's important is if you have an idea, don't just sit back. Get up and do it. It's not a problem to sometimes ask how to go about it. But be careful who you go to. There are people who will discourage you. So who is the right person? Your social network matters. Make sure you surround yourself with people who encourage and inspire you. If you don't try, you'll never know. We all have to start from somewhere.

Nkandu: What inspires you?

Fauza: Passion inspires me. We moved to Dubai in 2011 because of my husband's new job. The city is full of energy, day and night, and it tells you to get up and do something. There are inspirations everywhere, so it's the creativity, the country, the expat life. I do what I do because I love it. I never feel tired when I have a client coming over. I always tell myself I can juggle it all. To work on what's important and find balance. Then everything else will fall into place. If you find that balance, you can do what you never thought yourself capable of.

Nkandu: Tell me about your company, BIF.

Fauza: I started Beltz Inspirations by Fauza (BIF) almost a year ago as a blog to share my ideas on décor and fashion, and then I thought of starting my own jewellery collection. It's been almost a year now, and the collection is doing well so far. I always have a new collection, and it's inspired by the Maasai of Kenya. I believe every woman needs something unique and intimate. I design and choose all of the pieces, and then I figure out how to mix the style and colour pallets. The mixing is done by woman in Kenya. It feels good to support them financially. That was one of the reasons I started BIF accessories. To do something for society in Kenya.

I'm also obsessed with posting it on social media. I feel a little guilty, because I'm just learning fashion, and I want to tell these women they don't have to struggle with it. It's not that difficult, because I believe it's not who you wear but what you wear. I always tell my clients it's important to dress for your body type. I don't want to brag, but if you put the simplest items together with a BIF necklace, you will look amazing.

Nkandu: You also have an interior design business.

Fauza: I call it more of a hobby. When we moved to Dubai, we were in this beautiful, big, empty, and echo-filled villa. That's when the passion started. I didn't want to just buy items and put them together, because I'd be creating a showroom rather than a home. I started taking design workshops before I moved to short courses. Then I went back to school to get a diploma in Interior Design. I already have clients. I get people who ask for my advice, but I'm just freelancing. My key message is that you don't have to work hard or spend a lot of money to have a beautiful home. It's the simple things that make the difference.

Nkandu: Do you have any quotes you'd like to share?

Fauza: I do have some favourite quotes. One is by Oprah Winfrey. She says, 'If you don't know what your passion is, realise that one reason for your existence on earth is to find it.' Then there's one I'm obsessed with by Bill Rancic. He always says, 'you don't have to be the smartest person in the world. All you need to do is work hard and believe in what you're doing.' Another one is by Louise Hay. She says, 'Don't be afraid to be you. The world needs your unique brand of awesomeness.'

Fauza Beltz is a co-author of *Fierce and Fabulous: The Feminine Force of Success.*

About Fierce and Fabulous:
The Feminine Force of Success

'With every experience, you alone are painting your own canvas, thought by thought, choice by choice.'

Oprah Winfrey

'Our deepest fear is not that we are inadequate, our deepest fear is that we are powerful beyond measure... We ask ourselves, who am I to be brilliant, gorgeous, talented and fabulous?'

Marianne Williamson

RISING FROM THE DUST

*'Never underestimate what an individual
with a powerful thought can do!'*

Nkandu Beltz

Fierce and Fabulous shares the reality of what it means for women in business today, and how adversity can become a driving force for business, community, and change.

- Are you a woman who wants more?

- Are you searching for success?

- Is your life running on love or fear?

In this book, we have a deeper conversation with women about:

- The real issues women in business are facing

- How to go from Struggle Street to Success Avenue

- How to overcome adversities so you can live your dreams.

YOU ARE Extraordinary!

Fierce and Fabulous is a dedication to the lives and achievements of extraordinary women who are changing the world. This is a collection of the stories of inspirational women.

Featuring: Chantal Harris, Eva Sifis, Fauza Beltz, Fur Wale, Gaye O'Brien, Jacinta Petrie, Kelly Fletcher, Kia Dowell, Philippa Ross, Rebecca McIntyre, Sharron Keating, Suzanne Waldron, Tania de Jong, Therese Howell, Rebecca McIntyre and Yeukai Ota.

www.fierceandfabulous.com.au

ABOUT THE AUTHOR
Fauza Beltz

Fauza is the founder of BIF Design. Beltz Inspirations by Fauza, consists of all her creativity in interior design as well as her Jewelry collection. Born in a rural part of Kwale in Kenya, Fauza acquired her Dutch citizenship after marrying the love of her life. Fauza has one child, Jasper. She is a qualified interior designer from the Centre of Executive Education Dubai and a jewellery designer.

BIF Design is a blog about fashion, interior design and her jewellery collection. This blog aims to inspire people and empower women in Kenya who make the jewellery and which is sold through the BIF website.

Fauza has a background in customer service, sales and marketing and public relations. She has worked as a customer service representative for Panari Hotel in Nairobi, Kenya. Her passion lies in decorating comfortable spaces that are not only beautiful but practical to the people living there.

In 2015 Fauza had the privilege to be one of the Ro'Ya participants, a Dubai Business Women Council and MasterCard initiative to empower and encourage female entrepreneurs in the United Arab Emirates.

She has co-authored *Fierce and Fabulous: The Feminine Force of Success.*

In 2016 Fauza was awarded The Feminine Force of Success Award for being resilient and hard working.

Fauza lives in Dubai in the United Arab Emirates with her husband and son.

Do you need help in turning your house into home?

Do you feel like you need help with your sense of Fashion? Are you struggling with mix and match?

As a creative person I strongly believe that it's the simple things that can make a huge difference. Be it in your home décor or even on your dress code. So often people struggle not knowing how to put things together.

As a consultant I can help you in finding your authentic self.

Let me sort your home with a style that suits you and your family.

I would love to accessorise your outfits. Each piece of my jewelry is handmade to suit all the different women. Each necklace has its own beauty. Help me in supporting other women back in Africa.

fauzabeltz@gmail.com

www.fauzabeltz.com

www.ingramcontent.com/pod-product-compliance
Lightning Source LLC
Chambersburg PA
CBHW021129300426
44113CB00006B/348